The Huckleberry
COOKBOOK

The Huckleberry
COOKBOOK

Second Edition

ALEX AND STEPHANIE HESTER

TWODOT®

GUILFORD, CONNECTICUT
HELENA, MONTANA

A · TWODOT® · BOOK

An imprint of Globe Pequot
A registered trademark of Rowman & Littlefield

Distributed by NATIONAL BOOK NETWORK

Copyright © 2017 by Rowman & Littlefield
All photos by Stephanie Hester except photos on pages 4, 17, 24, 37, 55, 74, 77, 86, 103, 106, 109, 113, 114, 116, 121, 122, and 125 by Robert Wilson
Cover image © The Picture Pantry / Alamy Stock Photo

British Library Cataloguing in Publication Information Available
Library of Congress Cataloging-in-Publication Data available

ISBN 978-1-4930-2836-8 (hardcover)
ISBN 978-1-4930-2837-5 (e-book)

♾™ The paper used in this publication meets the minimum requirements of American National Standard for Information Sciences—Permanence of Paper for Printed Library Materials, ANSI/NISO Z39.48-1992.

Printed in the United States of America

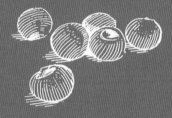

To Jack and Sam

And also to our multitalented family, who provided recipes, endless taste testing (no one is sick of huckleberries, yet), and critiques, tips, and photography for these recipes. Special thanks to Grandma Barb, Mom, Aunt Karen, and Uncle Rob.

Contents

Introduction

Like grizzly bears, glistening glacier-fed streams, and snow-capped mountaintops, huckleberries are an iconic western symbol—one that conjures up visions of pure wildness. They are one of nature's true delicacies, and in the West the wild huckleberry is prized above all other berries.

Wild is just one word to describe the huckleberry. It has also been described as distinctive, elusive, and erratic. These purple gems are distinctive because of their exclusivity, elusive because of their resistance to domestication and their preference for remote environments, and erratic because of their unpredictable yearly production. Prime huckleberry-picking spots are coveted secrets, and legends and lore about the fabled fruit have been around for centuries.

Henry David Thoreau was the first to comprehensively study the history of the huckleberry. His earliest findings about the fruit trace it back to 1615, when explorer Samuel de Champlain observed how Native Americans used the berry. Later, the Lewis and Clark journals documented Native American traditions of harvesting, drying, and preparing huckleberries, as well as sites where they encountered the berry on their expedition. On April 12, 1806, Captain William Clark wrote:

> The Indians left us about 6 P M and returned to their Village on the opposit Side. mountains are high on each Side and Covered with Snow for about ⅓ of the way down. the growth is principally fir and White Cedar. the bottoms and low Situations is Covered with a variety Such as Cotton, large leafed ash, Sweet willow a Species of beech, alder, white thorn, cherry of a Small Speces, Servis berry bushes, Huckleberries bushes, a Speces of Lorel & & I saw a turkey buzzard which is the 3rd which I have Seen west of the rocky mountains.

Traditional native uses for huckleberries included making dyes and teas for medicinal purposes, mixing them with meat to make a winter staple called "pemmican," mashing the berries and drying them in the sun to make cakes, and celebrating and honoring the berry in ceremonial rituals. Huckleberries were an important nutritional food source not only to natives but also to early settlers in the West throughout the nineteenth century.

In the early twentieth century, western settlers started to recognize the economic value of huckleberries, and fresh and canned berries began to be available for sale. During huckleberry season, families would travel high in the mountains to harvest berries. Although the primary purpose of these "working vacations" was to pick enough berries to last for family use through the winter, extras were picked and sold for profit.

By the mid-1920s, the once uncompromised berry harvest had been transformed into a large-scale commercial industry. Technological advances in food preservation (specifically canning), the availability of workers because of the shortage of jobs available during the Great Depression, and the development of forest service roads were all factors that precipitated the rapid growth in commercial huckleberry harvesting. Hundreds of eager pickers flocked to huckleberry camps during the 1930s, particularly in the area of northern Montana where huckleberries were abundant, due to the fires of 1910 that created prime growing conditions. Specialized harvesting tools were developed to maximize commercial harvesting. In 1937, regulation of the huckleberry industry was first instigated.

In the 1940s as general economic conditions improved, the commercial huckleberry camps began to decline. By 1950, the camps were a thing of the past, and the labor force shifted to the timber industry. Since the 1980s, however, there has been a resurgence in the use of huckleberries as a regional product for the tourism market. Today, one can easily purchase a multitude of huckleberry goods, from jams and syrups to lotions and soaps.

Like blueberries, huckleberries contain high levels of antioxidants. This additional benefit may increase market demand in coming years, even as huckleberry production has been lower than average. Many believe the huckleberry has been overexploited at the expense of damaged plants and food shortages for wildlife. Land managers are now taxed with the responsibility of balancing the economic and cultural uses of the huckleberry, while residents and visitors continue to covet the fruit for cooking.

The Huckleberry Cookbook goes beyond customary huckleberry fare. Although we've included a handful of traditional recipes—including jam, pancakes, and pie—we've also incorporated the huckleberry into a variety of our favorite dishes and represented different cuisines. Some recipes bring out the full flavor of the huckleberry, while others utilize its flavor to complement or accent the other main ingredients. The truth is that huckleberries can accompany almost anything. Sidebars throughout the book explore different aspects of the berry's history, lore, and place in the West.

Although nothing could ever replace the huckleberry, blueberries are a good substitute for virtually any of the recipes included in this book. So if it's the middle of winter and you've depleted your huckleberry supply, you won't have to wait until summer to create the wonderful cuisine in this book.

Huckleberries are simply a treat. They are the essence of wildness in nature. Not sweet, not sour, they embody the perfect balance of flavor to scintillate the palate. This book contains an abundance of recipes to enjoy huckleberries in a variety of ways. But perhaps our favorite recipe happens to be the easiest to prepare: the field-dressed huckleberry—fresh and au naturel.

Breakfast and Brunch

Huckleberry Sour Cream Coffee Cake

We love this coffee cake and have made it with a variety of berries, including a mixture of blueberries, blackberries, and huckleberries. It is best served fresh.

Serves 8–12

BATTER

2 cups all-purpose flour

2 teaspoons baking powder

1 teaspoon baking soda

8 tablespoons (1 stick) unsalted butter, room temperature

¾ cup granulated sugar

1½ teaspoons vanilla extract

3 large eggs

2 cups sour cream

2 cups huckleberries

Preheat the oven to 350°F. Prepare a 9-inch springform pan or round cake pan with cooking spray or butter and flour. Combine the flour, baking powder, and baking soda together in a mixing bowl. Set aside. In a separate bowl, cream the butter, granulated sugar, and vanilla. Add the eggs, one at a time, and stir until the mixture is smooth and thoroughly mixed. Add the dry ingredients to butter mixture without over mixing. Fold in sour cream.

Spread half of the batter in the prepared pan. Layer the huckleberries on top. Spread remaining batter on top of the berries. Set aside while you prepare the crumble topping.

Blend brown sugar, flour, cinnamon, and butter with a fork or fingertips until it is well mixed and resembles coarse meal. Crumble the mixture evenly over the top layer of batter.

Bake for 30 to 40 minutes, until an inserted knife comes out clean. Cool and remove from pan.

CRUMBLE TOPPING

¼ cup firmly packed brown sugar

¼ cup all-purpose flour

½ teaspoon ground cinnamon

2 tablespoons (¼ stick) unsalted butter, room temperature

Gingerbread Huckleberry Pancakes

The basis for this family-favorite recipe came from a relative in Austin, Texas. Our huckleberry version adds a new dimension. For a healthy twist, you can combine white, whole wheat, rye, oat, or buckwheat flours.

Makes about 18 pancakes

Separate the egg yolks from the whites. With an electric mixer whip whites until stiff. In a separate bowl, combine flour, sugar, baking powder, baking soda, ground ginger, and salt. In a small bowl, mix the 2 egg yolks with the oil, buttermilk, and molasses until well blended. Combine the wet and dry ingredients until well blended. Fold in the whipped egg whites and then the huckleberries.

Butter or spray a griddle or large frying pan. Using approximately ¼ cup batter for each pancake gives a yield of 18 pancakes. Of course, the cook can make silver dollar size or larger size and the yield would vary accordingly. Cook over medium heat until both sides are golden brown and center is cooked. Top with maple syrup or your favorite huckleberry accompaniment. See Staples chapter.

2 large eggs

2 cups all-purpose flour

2 tablespoons sugar

2 teaspoons baking powder

1 teaspoon baking soda

½ teaspoon ground ginger

½ teaspoon salt

¼ cup vegetable oil

1¾ cups buttermilk

¼ cup light molasses

1 cup huckleberries

Huckleberry Buttermilk Pancakes

These are wonderfully light and fluffy pancakes. Top with Huckleberry Coulis (see page 132), Huckleberry Compote (see page 133), or your favorite topping.

Makes about 20 pancakes

2½ cups all-purpose flour

¼ cup sugar

2 teaspoons baking powder

2 teaspoons baking soda

1 teaspoon salt

2 cups buttermilk

2 cups sour cream

2 large eggs

4 teaspoons vanilla extract

2 cups huckleberries

Tip: No buttermilk in the fridge? You can make your own. Add 1 tablespoon vinegar or lemon juice to 1 cup of milk. Let sit for 10 minutes. Substitute this soured milk for buttermilk.

In a large mixing bowl, combine flour, sugar, baking powder, baking soda, and salt. In a separate small mixing bowl, whisk together buttermilk, sour cream, eggs, and vanilla, and add to the dry ingredients. Stir until ingredients are just mixed, making sure not to overmix. Fold in huckleberries. Butter or spray a griddle or large frying pan. Use a ¼ cup to measure out each pancake. Cook over medium heat, several minutes per side until golden brown and cooked through.

What's in a Name: Taxonomy and Species Identification

Is it a huckleberry, hurtleberry, blueberry, bilberry, dewberry, or whortleberry? The huckleberry has been called by many names and is frequently misidentified and most often mistaken for the blueberry. However, there are several features that distinguish the huckleberry from all others.

To the connoisseur, taste is the predominant distinction. Although passionate blueberry lovers will likely disagree, "blah!" is what many people say when they compare the taste of a blueberry to a huckleberry. The flavor of the huckleberry has endless body, whereas blueberries are comparatively plain.

Thirty-five to forty species of huckleberries exist in North America. Related to the blueberry and the cranberry, the huckleberry belongs to the genus *Vaccinium* and can be found in remote areas of Washington, Oregon, Idaho, Montana, and British Columbia. Most huckleberry connoisseurs agree that the tastiest species are globe (or blue) huckleberries (*Vaccinium globulare*) and mountain (or big) huckleberries (*Vaccinium membranaceum*).

Depending on the species, huckleberry bushes grow anywhere from one and a half feet to five feet tall and have brown or light green branches. The green leaves

of a huckleberry bush are oval shaped and about two and a half inches long. Huckleberry blossoms are bell shaped and usually a whitish-pink color. The berries vary in color, from purples and deep purplish blacks to blues and reds. Typically about the size of a pea, they have smooth skin and a depression at the tip where the flower was. Blueberries tend to be larger and have a more pronounced, scalloped depression. Huckleberries tend to grow widely separated on the plant, whereas blueberries grow in clumps. With a wonderfully pungent smell, the odor of huckleberries is so strong it can permeate plastic bags. (As such, double bagging is recommended when freezing.) Some pickers claim to find productive huckleberry patches by simply following the aromatic scent of the huckleberry.

If you are hunting huckleberries for the first time, we suggest that you obtain a field guide that identifies and describes the specific species in the area you will be foraging.

Bread Pudding with Huckleberry Compote

This is definitely an indulgent breakfast, but you can serve this anytime of the day. It's particularly tasty in the afternoon with a good, strong cup of tea or coffee.

Serves 6–8

4 cups of any day-old bread, cut into 1-inch cubes

¼ cup walnuts, chopped

4 large eggs

1 cup packed brown sugar

2½ cups milk

2 tablespoons vanilla extract

2 tablespoons ground cinnamon

¼ cup (½ stick) unsalted butter, melted

Huckleberry Compote (see page 133)

Prepare a 13 x 9 x 2-inch baking dish with cooking spray or butter and flour. Place bread and walnuts in the prepared dish. In an electric blender, combine the eggs, brown sugar, milk, vanilla, cinnamon, and butter. Blend well. Pour mixture over bread and walnuts. Cover and refrigerate for up to 24 hours.

When ready to bake, preheat the oven to 350°F. Bake for 50 minutes, or until the center is firm. Let stand for 10 minutes. Serve warm with huckleberry compote.

Berry Yogurt Parfait

We prefer this dish with vanilla yogurt, but feel free to choose your favorite flavor. You can also substitute Shredded Wheat, Grape-Nuts, or any other crunchy cereal for the granola. Use whatever berries you have on hand, or prepare it with Zested Berry Medley with Chambord (see page 145).

Makes 1 serving

In a parfait glass, layer the yogurt, granola, and berries, and enjoy.

1 cup vanilla yogurt

½ cup of your favorite granola

¼ cup huckleberries

¼ cup blueberries

¼ cup strawberries, cut and hulled

Huckleberry Strata

Bursting with rich flavor, this is a great dish for Sunday brunch. It's quick to make and can be prepared up to 24 hours in advance.

Serves 8–12

2½ cups huckleberries

1 cup huckleberry preserves

8 large eggs

2½ cups milk

2 tablespoons (¼ stick) unsalted butter, melted

¼ cup maple syrup

1 tablespoon almond extract

1 teaspoon ground cinnamon

1 teaspoon grated or ground nutmeg

½ teaspoon ground ginger

6 large croissants, cut in half lengthwise

1 (8-ounce) package cream cheese, cut into ½-inch cubes

1 cup toasted almonds

Prepare a 13 x 9 x 2-inch baking dish with cooking spray or butter and flour. In a heavy saucepan combine huckleberries and preserves. Heat on low until well mixed and the huckleberries are cooked down, about 10 minutes. Set aside.

In an electric blender combine the eggs, milk, butter, syrup, almond extract, and spices. Blend until the mixture is frothy. Set aside.

Layer 6 croissant halves in the prepared dish. Evenly distribute the cream cheese cubes over the croissants. Pour the huckleberry mixture over the cream cheese. Top with another layer of croissants. Pour the egg mixture evenly over the croissants. Using a spatula or spoon, gently press on croissants to moisten them. Cover and refrigerate overnight.

When ready to bake, preheat the oven to 325°F. Place the strata on the center rack in the oven and bake for 35 to 40 minutes, or until the top is golden brown and the egg mixture is set. Remove from the oven and let stand for 10 minutes. Top with almonds.

Huck Kuchen

A version of kuchen was brought to the United States by Stephanie's great-grandmother when she emigrated as a German from Russia in the early twentieth century. Using huckleberries is a new twist on this family treat. This recipe is not difficult but does require planning ahead, as both the dough and pastry cream are refrigerated overnight. It is worth the effort, however, and can be made with other fruits in addition to huckleberries. Thanks to Karen Wilson for contributing the history, recipe, and photo for this delish family tradition.

2 9" pie pans (square or pie)

DOUGH

½ cup plus 2 tablespoons whole milk

½ envelope active dry yeast (1⅛ teaspoons)

½ large egg (2 tablespoons)

2 cups all-purpose flour, plus more for rolling

2 tablespoons plus 1½ teaspoons sugar

½ teaspoon salt

6 tablespoons (¾ stick) unsalted butter, room temperature

DOUGH

Heat the milk to 110°F and transfer it to a small bowl. Stir in the yeast and let stand for 5 minutes, until dissolved. Stir in the egg. Using a stand mixer fitted with a dough hook, mix the 2 cups of flour with the sugar and salt; add the warm milk mixture and knead at medium-low speed until a stiff dough forms, about 3 minutes. Add the softened butter and knead at medium speed until the dough is silky and soft, about 5 minutes. Transfer the dough to a buttered bowl, cover with plastic wrap, and refrigerate overnight.

PASTRY CREAM

2 tablespoons all-purpose flour

¼ cup sugar

¾ cup whole milk

1 large egg

½ teaspoon vanilla extract

3 cups huckleberries

TOPPING

¼ cup plus 2 tablespoons sugar

1½ tablespoons all-purpose flour

1½ tablespoons unsalted butter, room temperature

Pinch of ground cinnamon

PASTRY CREAM

In a medium bowl, combine the flour with 2 tablespoons of the sugar and 2 tablespoons of the milk and whisk to a paste. Whisk in the egg and vanilla. In a medium saucepan, heat the remaining ½ cup plus 2 tablespoons of milk and 2 tablespoons of sugar over moderate heat until the sugar is dissolved. Gradually whisk the hot milk into the egg mixture. Cook the mixture in the saucepan over moderate heat, whisking constantly, until thickened and no floury taste remains, about 4 minutes. Transfer the pastry cream to a bowl and cover with plastic wrap, pressing it directly onto the surface to prevent a skin from forming. Refrigerate overnight.

ASSEMBLE THE KUCHEN

Preheat the oven to 350°F.

Butter two 9-inch pie plates (or other comparably sized baking dishes) with butter. Divide dough into two pieces and flatten into disks (the dough will be firm). On a lightly floured work surface, roll out each disk of dough to a 9½-inch round. Place each round in a prepared pie plate, making sure that the dough doesn't extend past the rims. Cover the pie plates with plastic wrap and let stand at room temperature until the dough has risen slightly, about 1 hour.

While the dough is rising, make the topping. In a small bowl, combine the sugar with the flour and butter and run with your fingers until the texture is sandy.

After the dough has risen slightly, lightly press the dough with your fingers to deflate any bubbles. Arrange the huckleberries on the dough in a single layer. Spread the pastry cream evenly over the huckleberries.

Then sprinkle the topping over the pastry cream and dust lightly with cinnamon.

Bake the kuchens for 40 minutes, until the crusts are deeply golden. Transfer the kuchens to a rack to cool. The kuchens may be served warm or at room temperature (personal preference). The baked kuchens can be wrapped in foil and frozen for up to 1 month.

Breads, Muffins, and Pastries

Huckleberry Bread

Delicious any season, this bread is especially good comfort food in the fall and winter. Remember to freeze berries in season to make a loaf or two when fresh huckleberries aren't available. Or prepare this in the summer and freeze a baked loaf for later.

Makes 1 standard loaf

2 cups all-purpose flour

¾ cup sugar

3 teaspoons baking powder

¼ teaspoon salt

2 large eggs

1 cup whole milk

1 teaspoon vanilla extract

3 tablespoons vegetable oil

1 cup huckleberries

½ cup chopped walnuts or pecans (optional)

Preheat the oven to 350°F. Prepare a 9 x 5-inch loaf pan with cooking spray or butter and flour. Combine flour, sugar, baking powder, and salt in a large mixing bowl. In a separate bowl, whisk the eggs and then add milk, vanilla, and oil. Add the egg mixture to the dry ingredients without overmixing. Fold in the huckleberries and nuts, if desired. Pour the batter into prepared pan. Bake for 1 hour, or until an inserted knife pulls out clean. Let cool completely and remove from pan.

Huckleberry Banana Bread

This is a moist, delicious banana bread, and the addition of huckleberries gives it a distinctive, fresh taste.

Makes 1 loaf

Preheat the oven to 350°F. Prepare a 9 x 5-inch loaf pan with cooking spray or butter and flour. In a large bowl and using an electric mixer, cream the butter and sugar. Mix in eggs and vanilla. Next, add flour, baking soda, and salt. Mix well. Add bananas and mix until all ingredients are well blended. Fold in the huckleberries and almonds, if desired. Pour the batter into the loaf pan. Bake 1 hour, or until an inserted knife pulls out clean. Let cool completely and remove from pan.

⅓ cup unsalted butter

1 cup sugar

2 large eggs

½ teaspoon vanilla extract

1½ cups all-purpose flour

1 teaspoon baking soda

1 teaspoon salt

4 ripe bananas, mashed

½ cup huckleberries

½ cup chopped almonds (optional)

Huckleberry Lemon Scones

Like the traditional British scone, these are not particularly sweet. To satisfy a sweet tooth, you can coat all sides with raw sugar before baking rather than just sprinkling it on the top.

Makes 12 scones

3 cups all-purpose flour, plus more for rolling

⅓ cup granulated sugar

2½ teaspoons baking powder

1 teaspoon salt

½ teaspoon baking soda

1 tablespoon freshly grated lemon zest

¾ cup (1½ sticks) unsalted butter, chilled and cut into ½-inch cubes

¾ cup huckleberries

1 cup buttermilk

3 tablespoons raw sugar

Preheat the oven to 400°F. In a large mixing bowl, combine the flour, granulated sugar, baking powder, salt, and baking soda. Mix in the lemon zest. Add the butter. Mix ingredients with a pastry cutter or your fingertips until the mixture resembles coarse meal. Carefully mix in the huckleberries. Gradually add buttermilk, tossing with fork until moist clumps form. Do not overmix.

Transfer the dough to a lightly floured work surface. Softly knead the dough to bind it, only about four turns. Form the dough into 1-inch-thick log. Cut the log in a V shape, making about 12 wedges. Sprinkle the tops with sugar. Transfer the scones to a baking sheet, spacing them evenly. Bake 18 to 20 minutes, or until the tops of the scones are golden brown. Remove from the oven and let cool.

Healthy Huckleberry Banana Muffins

These may be healthier than your average muffin, but they are just as satisfying.

Makes 12 muffins

1½ cups whole wheat flour

¼ cup oat bran

½ cup sugar

2 teaspoons baking powder

½ teaspoon salt

3 ripe bananas, mashed

½ cup soy milk

1 large egg

2 tablespoons vegetable oil

2 teaspoons lemon juice

1 cup huckleberries

Preheat the oven to 400°F. Prepare muffin tins with paper liners or spray them with cooking oil. In a medium mixing bowl, combine the flour, oat bran, sugar, baking powder, and salt. In a separate large mixing bowl, combine the bananas, milk, egg, oil, and lemon juice. Add the dry ingredients without overmixing. Fold in the huckleberries. Fill the muffin cups about two-thirds full. Bake 20 minutes, or until an inserted knife or cake tester pulls out clean. Remove from pan and cool.

Huckleberry Season

Huckleberry season is relatively brief—far too brief for those who patiently wait for them each summer and who miscalculated their needs the previous year. In general, the first berries begin to ripen in late July and flourish through the beginning of September. A host of conditions, including climatic variations, altitude, location, and plant species, dictate the length of the season  each year, as well as the production. In some years a bush will produce only a couple cups of berries, and in other years a gallon of berries can be collected from the same bush.

We have witnessed early blooms the past couple of years and crop yields from boomers to undersize berries. Climate change is likely a factor in the shift to an earlier season and erratic yields, so we'll see what the future brings.

In September 2016, I spoke with someone who saw huckleberries in full bloom at about 6,500 feet in northern Idaho. Just like most things, timing is everything with huckleberry picking. You just have to be in the know.

During the season, huckleberries are available at farmers' markets across the West. Some of these sellers may be using commercial harvesting techniques that are ecologically unsound, so we recommend that you check with your local providers about their picking philosophy.

Huckleberry Corn Muffins

Hearty and just barely sweet, this muffin can accompany either your breakfast cereal or a bowl of chili.

Makes 18 muffins

1½ cups all-purpose flour

½ cup whole wheat flour

½ cup cornmeal

¾ cup sugar

2½ teaspoons baking powder

½ teaspoon baking soda

½ teaspoon salt

½ cup buttermilk

½ cup orange juice

¼ cup (½ stick) unsalted butter, melted

1 large egg, beaten

1 tablespoon freshly grated orange zest

2 cups huckleberries

Preheat the oven to 400°F. Prepare muffin tins with paper liners or spray them with cooking oil. In a large bowl, combine the flours, cornmeal, sugar, baking powder, baking soda, and salt. In a separate bowl, whisk together the buttermilk, orange juice, butter, egg, and orange zest. Add to dry ingredients, mixing until just moistened. Fold in the huckleberries. Spoon the batter into the prepared muffin cups, filling each about two-thirds full. Bake for 20 to 25 minutes, or until an inserted knife or cake tester pulls out clean.

Huckleberry Soda Bread

Here's a nod to our Irish heritage. Typically prepared with raisins, dried berries, or dried fruit, huckleberries update this traditional Irish quick bread and add a new dimension to an old favorite.

Makes 1 loaf

Preheat the oven to 375°F. Prepare an 8-inch baking pan with cooking spray or butter and flour. In a medium mixing bowl, combine the flour, sugar, baking powder, baking soda, and salt. Stir in the buttermilk and oil until just mixed. Fold in the huckleberries.

Transfer the dough to a lightly floured work surface. Softly knead it to bind the dough, only a couple of turns. Shape into a 6-inch round and place it in the prepared pan. With a knife, score the top of the dough with an X. Place the pan on the center rack in the oven and bake for 40 minutes, or until the top is golden brown. Remove from the oven and generously brush the top with melted butter. This is best served warm.

2 cups all-purpose flour, plus more for rolling

2 tablespoons sugar

2 teaspoons baking powder

¼ teaspoon baking soda

½ teaspoon sea salt

1 cup buttermilk

¼ cup vegetable oil

½ cup huckleberries

3 tablespoons unsalted butter, melted

Huckleberry Beignets

We fell in love with these deep-fried fritters on a trip to New Orleans. In this version the Big Easy meets the Rocky Mountains in an indulgent, scrumptious treat.

Makes about 20 beignets

2 large eggs

1½ cups all-purpose flour

¾ cup milk

1 tablespoon granulated sugar

1 teaspoon baking powder

¼ teaspoon salt

1 cup huckleberries

Vegetable oil

½ cup confectioners' sugar

In a large mixing bowl, whisk the eggs until light and fluffy. Add the flour, milk, granulated sugar, baking powder, and salt. Whisk well, making a smooth batter. Fold in the huckleberries.

Fill a large deep pot or electric deep fryer about halfway up with vegetable oil. Heat on high to 360°F.

Gently drop about 6 heaping tablespoons of batter, one at a time, into the hot oil. Be careful not to overcrowd the pot. Fry and turn the beignets until they are evenly brown on all sides, about 2–3 minutes. Remove the beignets from the oil and place them on paper towels to drain. Sprinkle with confectioners' sugar. These are best served warm.

Huckleberry Cream Cheese Tartlets

The key to making these pastries look as good as they taste is to work quickly and carefully with the phyllo dough and to crimp the edges together decoratively and firmly so the filling doesn't leak out.

Makes 8 tartlets

Preheat the oven to 350°F. Make two stacks of 4 phyllo sheets each on a flat work surface. Fold one stack lightly in half lengthwise and brush the bottom sheet with butter and sprinkle with sugar. Peel back the next half sheet and repeat. Repeat the process on the third half sheet. Do not butter and sugar the top layer. Repeat this process on the other side and then with the second stack. Spread the top layer of both stacks with preserves. Cut each stack into 4 squares.

Whisk together the cream cheese, sugar, zest, and egg. Place approximately 1 tablespoon of cheese mixture in the center of each square. Place 1 tablespoon of the compote on top of the cheese. Pull up all four corners of the phyllo dough and twist them together, forming a free-form cup. Place them on an ungreased baking sheet.

Bake for 12 to 15 minutes, until the phyllo is browned and crispy. Let cool before serving.

8 sheets phyllo dough, thawed

4 tablespoons (½ stick) unsalted butter, melted

2 tablespoons sugar

4 tablespoons huckleberry preserves

FILLING

1 (8-ounce) package cream cheese, room temperature

6 tablespoons sugar

1 tablespoon freshly grated lemon zest

1 large egg

Huckleberry Compote (see page 133)

The Polebridge Merc
and the Huckleberry Bear Claw

Nestled snugly between the dusty North Fork Road ten miles south of the Canadian border and the wild North Fork River just west of Glacier National Park's rugged peaks that serve as a jagged backdrop to Polebridge, Montana, the Polebridge Mercantile & Bakery (the Merc) is a beacon for off-the-beaten-path floaters, boaters, anglers and other assorted folks who wander through Polebridge.

The Merc treats its patrons like kings (in the wilderness) by providing a variety of sundries, from toiletries to ice and local souvenirs. But beyond that, the Merc is renowned for its homemade baked goods and offerings. Most important to most, including the authors, is its Huckleberry Bear Claw.

The only true way to experience this filling and rich pastry is to enjoy it on the Merc grounds (either sitting on the porch or marveling at the mountains), so it's not worth sensationalizing the claw too much here. The Merc is accessible and open all year-round.

Note: For those of you a little less adventurous, a new and tamer outlet of the Merc is now open in Whitefish, Montana, about an hour and a half south.

Spongy Huckleberry Muffins

Yummy. Quick. Easy. These muffins can be made in a snap and maintain their moistness for a few days, thanks to the yogurt.

Makes 12–18 muffins

Preheat the oven to 385°F. In a large bowl sift together the flour, baking soda, baking powder, salt, and nutmeg. Set aside. In another large bowl, whisk together the granulated sugar, oil, vanilla, egg, and yogurt.

Mix dry and wet ingredients. Add 1½ cups huckleberries, reserving ½ cup, to the mixture and stir three times.

Prepare muffin tins with liners or cooking spray and fill two-thirds full with batter. Evenly divide the remaining berries on top and press them lightly into the batter. Sprinkle turbinado sugar over top. Bake 20 to 25 minutes; allow to cool completely before serving.

3 cups minus 2 tablespoons all-purpose flour

1 teaspoon baking soda

2 teaspoons baking powder

Heavy pinch of salt

Dash of grated nutmeg

1 cup granulated sugar

½ cup vegetable oil

1 teaspoon vanilla extract

1 egg

1 generous cup plain yogurt (We like using lemon flavored)

2 cups fresh huckleberries

Turbinado sugar (optional)

Baked Huckleberry Doughnut Holes

Here's a sweet little treat that is sure to please.

Makes 48 mini doughnut holes

2¾ cups all-purpose flour

¼ cup cornstarch

2¼ cups sugar, divided

1 tablespoon baking powder

½ teaspoon grated or ground nutmeg

1 teaspoon salt

1 cup buttermilk

1⅛ cups (2¼ sticks) unsalted butter, melted and divided

2 large eggs plus 1 egg yolk

1 cup huckleberries

2½ teaspoons ground cinnamon

Preheat oven to 400°F. Prepare mini muffin tins with liners or cooking spray for 48 doughnuts. In a large bowl, combine the flour, cornstarch, 1 cup sugar, baking powder, nutmeg, and salt. In a separate bowl, whisk the buttermilk, ½ cup melted butter, eggs, and yolk. Combine the dry and wet ingredients, mixing just until incorporated—don't overmix. Gently fold in the huckleberries. Drop approximately 1 tablespoon batter into each prepared mini cup.

Bake for 10 minutes, or until light brown and a toothpick inserted in the center comes out clean. Remove from the pans and let cool.

Meanwhile, combine the remaining 1¼ cups sugar with the cinnamon in a small bowl.

Using a pastry brush coat the entire doughnut with the remaining melted butter. Roll each doughnut in the cinnamon sugar mixture, packing it on.

Let rest. Enjoy. These doughnuts freeze well.

Huckleberry Cream Boho Rolls

These Boho rolls originate from Baltic countries, which includes Bohemia (a region in the Czech Republic). Known as kolacy or kolache, Balkans brought them to the United States about 1840. Huckleberries are a new flavor for these old rolls.

Makes 12 rolls

PASTRY

½ package dry yeast (1 teaspoon plus ⅛ teaspoon dry yeast)

¼ cup warm water

3 tablespoons plus ½ teaspoon sugar, divided

⅜ cup (6 tablespoons) evaporated milk or cream

2 tablespoons (¼ stick) unsalted butter, melted

2 tablespoons vegetable shortening, melted

2 large egg yolks (separate whites for egg washing rolls)

¼ teaspoon salt

2 cups all-purpose flour, plus more for rolling

Stir the yeast, water, and ½ teaspoon sugar together in a small bowl and set aside until it starts to bubble (about 15 minutes). In a separate bowl mix together all remaining pastry ingredients except the flour. Add this to the yeast mixture. Slowly stir in flour. A soft dough will form.

On a lightly floured work surface, knead the dough for about 5 minutes until smooth. Shape into a ball. Oil a bowl, making sure to coat all sides and place the ball of dough into the bowl. Set in a warm spot and cover until it is doubled in bulk, about 1 hour.

Once doubled in size, deflate the dough. Form into 12 equal-size balls. Flatten each into a circle 3 inches in diameter. Place them on parchment-lined baking sheets; you can use two 11 x 17 baking/cookie sheets and place 6 rolls on each sheet. That allows them to be spaced approximately 2 inches apart. Cover with a tea towel and let rise until doubled in size, 40 minutes to 1 hour.

Meanwhile, combine all the cheese filling ingredients except the jam in a small bowl. Blend together with a hand mixer until smooth. Stir in the huckleberry jam. There should be an additional amount of jam to top the rolls. 1–2 tablespoons of jam is mixed with the cheese filling. Then after the cheese filling is placed on the rolls, another ½ tsp. of jam is added to the top (6 more tsp. of jam for the 12 rolls).

Mix all *posepka* ingredients together in a small bowl until crumbly.

When the rolls are doubled in size, make a depression in the center of each, fill it with cheese filling, and top the filling with huckleberry jam. Beat the reserved egg whites with a fork and using a pastry brush, brush the exposed pastry with the beaten egg whites.

Then sprinkle each roll with posepka and bake at 375°F. for 15–20 minutes or until edges of rolls are a golden brown. Cool on a baking rack. The rolls can be wrapped in foil or placed in freezer bags and frozen for up to 1 month.

CHEESE FILLING

8 ounces cream cheese, room temperature

¼ cup sugar

3 tablespoons all-purpose flour

1 large egg yolk

½ teaspoon finely grated lemon zest

1–2 tablespoons huckleberry jam, plus 6 more teaspoons for topping rolls

POSEPKA (FOR TOP OF ROLLS)

3 tablespoons all-purpose flour

3 tablespoons sugar

1 tablespoon unsalted butter, room temperature

Zucchini Huckleberry Bread with Lemon Glaze

In this recipe, classic zucchini bread is improved with the purple gems exploding inside. The lemon glaze is not essential, unless you want to sweeten this moist quick bread with a little citrus flavor.

Makes 2 loaves

Preheat the oven to 350°F. Lightly grease two standard loaf pans, 9¼ x 5¼ inch. In a large bowl, beat together the eggs, oil, vanilla, and sugar. Fold in the zucchini. Stir in the flour, salt, baking powder, and baking soda. Gently fold in the huckleberries. Pour the batter evenly between the prepared loaf pans.

Bake for 45 minutes, or until a toothpick inserted in the center comes out clean. Cool for 20 minutes in pan and transfer to wire racks to cool completely.

To make the lemon glaze, combine all ingredients until thoroughly mixed. Pour glaze over loaves while still warm as they cool on the racks. Slice when the loaves are cooled and the glaze is set.

3 large eggs

1 cup vegetable oil

1 tablespoon vanilla extract

2¼ cups sugar

2 cups shredded zucchini

3 cups all-purpose flour

1 teaspoon salt

1 teaspoon baking powder

½ teaspoon baking soda

2 cups fresh or frozen huckleberries

LEMON GLAZE (OPTIONAL)

1 cup confectioners' sugar

1 tablespoon lemon juice

1 tablespoon half-and-half or heavy whipping cream

Appetizers, Salads, and Sides

Huckleberry Dragon Wings

Spicy with a hint of sweet, these aren't your ordinary wings.

Serves 6–8

DRAGON SAUCE

¼ cup soy sauce

2 tablespoons rice vinegar

1 tablespoon sesame oil

1 clove garlic, peeled and grated

1 tablespoon fresh ginger, grated

1 tablespoon sambal (freshly ground chile paste)

¼ cup fresh huckleberries

CHICKEN WINGS

2 pounds whole chicken wings

Canola or peanut oil, for frying

½ cup sliced green onions

2 tablespoons toasted sesame seeds

Prepare the sauce by placing all sauce ingredients into a blender. Puree until smooth. Pour into a small saucepan and simmer until slightly reduced. Set aside.

Separate the wings by chopping them into sections at the joints. Discard the wing tips. Rinse the wings and pat dry.

Heat the oil in a deep pot, to prevent splattering, to 360°F. Fry the wings in batches, so not to overcrowd the pot, for 12 to 15 minutes, or until golden brown. Remove them from the oil and place on a paper-towel-lined baking sheet to drain any excess oil. Transfer the wings to a bowl and toss with the sauce. Place them on a platter and garnish with green onions and toasted sesame seeds. Serve either hot or cold.

Baked Brie en Croute with Huckleberry Chutney

Fresh out of the oven, baked brie is a succulent hors d'oeuvre—especially when accompanied by this savory chutney.

Serves 10

Preheat the oven to 350°F. Stack the phyllo sheets on a flat work surface. Fold lightly in half lengthwise and brush the bottom sheet with butter. Peel back the next half sheet and brush with butter; repeat until you reach the top layer. Repeat this process on the other side.

Once each layer is buttered, place the brie on the center of the stack. Pull up the edges of the phyllo around the brie and seal with your fingers. Brush with butter, turn over, and transfer it to a baking sheet. Brush the top to coat with butter to liking with the remaining butter. Bake for 15 to 20 minutes, or until golden. Place on a serving platter and garnish with the chutney, either spooning it over the top or placing it on the side. Serve with crackers or sliced French bread.

5 sheets phyllo dough, work with it out of freezer until pliable

4 tablespoons (½ stick) unsalted butter, melted

1 (6-inch) round of brie

Huckleberry Chutney (see page 139)

Roast Beef with Huckleberry Horseradish on Crostini

This is a versatile hors d'oeuvre for almost any occasion.

Serves 6–8

CROSTINI

1 baguette

¼ cup olive oil

4 cloves garlic, peeled and halved

TOPPING

½ pound deli-sliced roast beef

Huckleberry Horseradish (see page 143)

1 bunch chives, finely chopped, for garnish

Preheat the oven to 425°F. Slice the baguette into ½-inch-thick rounds. Place the rounds on a baking sheet and brush both sides with oil. Rub each piece with the cut side of a garlic clove. Bake 5 to 7 minutes, or until golden brown and crispy. Remove from oven and cool.

Place a small amount of roast beef on each crostini. Top the roast beef with a small dollop of huckleberry horseradish. Garnish with chives.

Turkey Pinwheels with Huckleberry Cream Cheese

Here's a quick snack or a hearty appetizer for kids and adults alike.

Serves 8–10

Place the tortillas on a flat work surface. Spread approximately 2 tablespoons of cream cheese on each tortilla. Layer approximately ½ cup greens over the cream cheese on each tortilla. Dividing them equally, layer the turkey and cheese on top of the greens. Roll tightly. Slice in 1½- to 2-inch rounds and serve.

4 large tortillas or wraps

½ cup Huckleberry Cream Cheese Spread, room temperature (see page 140)

2 cups mixed greens

½ pound deli-sliced turkey

½ pound thinly sliced cheese

Vichyssoise with Huckleberry Swirl

This French potato-leek soup is served cold. The potato and huckleberry flavors complement each other nicely, and the contrasting colors present a visual treat, as well as a tasty one.

Serves 10–12

SOUP

1 tablespoon unsalted butter

2 large leeks, washed thoroughly and coarsely chopped

1 sweet medium onion, chopped

¾ cup dry white wine

4 medium Yukon potatoes, peeled and diced

6 cups chicken broth

4 whole cloves garlic

½ teaspoon salt

½ teaspoon white pepper

3 cups whole milk

Melt the butter in a large stockpot over medium-high heat. Add the leeks and onion, and stir for about 5 minutes, or until they are translucent but not yet brown. Add the wine and cook for 2 more minutes. Add the potatoes, broth, and garlic. Bring to a boil, cover, and then reduce the heat to medium-low and simmer for 40 minutes. (Adjust heat as required to keep a simmer.) Add the salt and pepper. Let the soup cool.

Once cool, puree the soup in a blender or food processor. Refrigerate for a minimum of 1 hour; overnight is best.

To prepare huckleberry swirl, place ¾ cup huckleberries (reserve ¼ cup for garnish), preserves, and cream in blender. Blend until well mixed and thickened.

Just before serving, add whole milk to soup. Blend for 15 seconds to aerate. Serve cold in chilled bowls. Place a dollop of huckleberry mixture onto the soup and use a knife to decoratively swirl it. Garnish with a few fresh berries.

HUCKLEBERRY SWIRL

1 cup huckleberries

2 tablespoons huckleberry preserves

½ cup heavy cream

Fresh Fruit Salad with Huckleberry Yogurt Dressing

Give an ordinary fruit salad some extra punch with this wonderful dressing.

Makes 1½ cups of dressing

YOGURT DRESSING

1 cup plain yogurt

¼ cup honey

Zest and juice of 1 lemon

½ cup fresh huckleberries

Freshly cracked black pepper

1 cup fresh fruit of your choice

Combine the yogurt, honey, lemon zest and juice, and huckleberries in an electric blender and mix well. Add black pepper to taste. Toss with your favorite combination of fresh fruits. Dressing can be kept in the refrigerator for up to one week.

Walnuts, Goat Cheese, and Mixed Greens with Huckleberry Vinaigrette

Makes 4 servings

Rinse and dry the greens and place them in a bowl. Toss with dressing to taste. Divide the greens among four salad plates. Crumble the goat cheese over the greens and sprinkle with huckleberries and walnuts.

12 ounces mixed greens

Huckleberry Vinaigrette (see page 136)

2 ounces goat cheese, crumbled

¼ cup fresh huckleberries

¼ cup chopped walnuts

Taming the Wild Huckleberry

One of the reasons huckleberries are such a precious commodity is that the wild huckleberry has not yet been domesticated—but not for a lack of trying. Although the idea of having access to huckleberries year-round is inviting, we hope the technology to cultivate or domesticate the huckleberry is never perfected. Mass production in its nonnative environment would diminish the berry's unique character, bold flavor, and individuality. This is precisely what happened to the blueberry when it was domesticated nearly two centuries ago. One can try to take the huckleberry out of the wild, but to maintain its integrity, you can't take the wild out of the huckleberry.

Huckleberry Chicken Salad

Chicken salad is often prepared with grapes or cranberries. We prefer huckleberries, which give this easy-to-make salad a fresh, distinctive taste.

Serves 4–6

In a medium bowl combine all ingredients except for the berries. Mix thoroughly. Fold in huckleberries. Cover and refrigerate for at least 30 minutes to let flavors blend. Serve over endive or other greens, or in a multigrain wrap.

2 cups cooked chicken breasts, cubed

½ cup sliced green onions (scallions)

¾ cup diagonally sliced celery

½ cup mayonnaise

1½ tablespoons apple cider vinegar

¼ cup chopped walnuts

2 teaspoons poppy seeds

1 teaspoon salt

1 cup fresh huckleberries

Roasted Potatoes with Thyme and Huckleberries

Huckleberries add a sweet and tart twist to this classic potato dish.

Serves 6–8

3 tablespoons olive oil

2 teaspoons sea salt

1 teaspoon freshly ground black pepper

2 teaspoons fresh chopped thyme

2 pounds fingerling potatoes (can substitute quartered sliced potatoes with the skins on)

1 red bell pepper, sliced

1 medium yellow onion, sliced

½ cup fresh huckleberries

Preheat the oven to 400°F. In a shallow 13 x 9 baking dish mix the oil, salt, pepper, and thyme. Toss the potatoes, bell pepper, and onion in the oil mixture, making sure to coat the vegetables well. Roast for 40 minutes. Remove the dish from the oven, stir, and increase heat to 450°F. Return the vegetables to the oven and cook for 15 minutes more. Sprinkle huckleberries over potatoes and cook for an additional 5 minutes.

Wedge Salad with Huckleberry Candied Bacon and Walnuts

Wedge salads can be pretty satisfying, so enjoy this as an entree or an appetizer, depending on your appetite.

Makes 1 cup of dressing

To make the dressing, mix crumbled blue cheese with the salt and pepper in a small bowl, breaking up any big chunks. Add the rest of the ingredients and blend well by hand depending on your desire for chunkiness. Refrigerate and keep up to 4 days.

For the salad, remove the core from the iceberg lettuce but otherwise keep it intact. Wash and dry the lettuce and then place it in refrigerator until chilled. Cut into quarters. When ready to serve, place quarter lettuce on plate, add dressing, then sprinkle with bacon and walnuts. Garnish with chives.

The dressing is also great with Huckleberry Dragon Wings (see page 44).

DRESSING

½ cup mild blue cheese
(Maytag recommended)

½ teaspoon salt

½ teaspoon freshly cracked black pepper

¼ cup buttermilk
(see the Tip on page 6)

¼ cup sour cream

¼ cup chopped scallions or chives

1 tablespoon lemon juice

SALAD

1 head iceberg lettuce

Huckleberry Candied Bacon (see page 144)

Toasted, chopped walnuts to taste

1 tablespoon chopped scallions or chives for garnish

Main Entrees

Huckleberry-Glazed Roast Chicken

The huckleberry glaze is a wonderful addition to a freshly roasted, moist chicken. In a pinch, you can whip up the glaze in no time and add it to a prepared store-brought roasted chicken.

Serves 4–6

GLAZE

½ cup white vinegar

½ cup (1 stick) unsalted butter

½ cup fresh or frozen huckleberries

1 teaspoon sugar

Salt and pepper to taste

ROAST CHICKEN

1 whole chicken (about 5 pounds)

¼ cup olive oil

2 cloves peeled garlic, finely chopped

Fresh rosemary sprigs

Salt and pepper

In a small saucepan over medium heat, combine the vinegar and butter. When the butter is melted, add the huckleberries and sugar. Reduce the heat to low and simmer for 10 minutes. Remove the saucepan from the heat and let cool. Put the cooled sauce in a blender or food processor, and puree until smooth. Return the sauce to the pan set over low heat to warm. Salt and pepper to taste. Set aside and prepare the chicken.

Preheat the oven to 400°F. Rinse the chicken and pat it dry. Place the chicken, breast side up, on a rack in a shallow roasting pan. Truss chicken (tie the legs together).

In a small bowl, whisk together the olive oil, chopped garlic, and rosemary. Add salt and pepper to taste. Generously coat the chicken with this mixture.

Place the roasting pan on the center rack in the oven. Roast, uncovered, for 90 minutes, or until a thermometer inserted into the thigh reads 180°F and the juice of the chicken is no longer pink when the thigh is pierced. Coat the chicken with two-thirds of the huckleberry glaze and cook 10 minutes more. Remove from the oven. Let stand for 15 minutes to redistribute juices.

After carving, spoon the remaining huckleberry glaze on the chicken for additional flavor and for presentation.

Tip: Use any leftover chicken to prepare Huckleberry Chicken Salad (see page 53).

Pan-Seared Salmon with Huckleberry Sauce

Producing a crispy crust is essential in this dish. The blend of huckleberries and basil is a perfect complement to the robust flavor of the salmon.

Serves 4

2 tablespoons olive oil

Salt and pepper

4 salmon fillets 6 oz.

⅓ cup water

1 cup fresh huckleberries

1 tablespoon sugar

Juice of 1 lemon

¼ cup finely chopped fresh basil

Heat a large skillet over high heat. Add the olive oil. Salt and pepper both sides of the salmon fillets. When the pan is hot, add the fillets, skin side down. Sear for approximately 4 minutes per side. Remove from the pan and let rest on a platter.

Reduce the heat to medium. In the same pan used to cook the fish, add the water and huckleberries. Simmer until huckleberries become tender about 5 minutes. Add the sugar and simmer 2 to 3 more minutes. Lastly, add lemon juice and basil, and stir. Remove the pan from the heat and let stand a few minutes. Drizzle the sauce over the salmon fillets.

Guide for Huckleberry Hounds

If you are looking for a map that reveals where to find the best huckleberry patches, look no further. One is not supplied in this book, and we're not sure one even exists. Pickers, berriers, or hounds—as they are called—are a private bunch when it comes to huckleberry locations.

Huckleberry picking is a labor-intensive, tedious process, but one that can be very rewarding and enjoyable and provide some solace. In general, huckleberries are found on steep slopes and in acidic soils at subalpine elevations above 3,500 feet. They are often prolific in burned areas that are ten to twenty years old, grow best in partial shade, and need sufficient moisture.

Huckleberries exist in bear country for bears, although there's enough for us humans, too. It's important to be respectful and attentive when foraging for berries. Further, we advocate that leave-no-trace principles be utilized when traveling through the wilderness in pursuit of berries. The delicate ecological balance and future sustainability of the huckleberry are at stake.

We believe handpicking is the only responsible method for collecting huckleberries. During the heyday of huckleberry camps in the 1930s, picking tools were handcrafted, including a variety of rakes and bush beaters (literally used to beat the berries off the bush). Although these mechanical harvesting tools increase yields and efficiency, they damage bushes, which leads to lower production in successive years.

Baby Back Ribs with Huckleberry Barbecue Sauce

This smoky and sweet barbecue sauce can be applied to any grilled meat.

Serves 4

HUCKLEBERRY BARBECUE SAUCE

½ medium sweet onion, chopped

2 fresh jalapeño peppers, chopped and seeded

5 cloves garlic, chopped

¼ cup white vinegar

¼ cup molasses

2 tablespoons huckleberry preserves

1 cup ketchup

1 tablespoon dry mustard

1 teaspoon granulated garlic

1 teaspoon granulated onion

1 teaspoon sweet paprika

1 teaspoon freshly ground black pepper

In a heavy saucepan over medium heat, sauté the onions, jalapeños, and garlic until soft. Add the vinegar, molasses, and huckleberry preserves. Simmer the mixture until everything is well incorporated about 5 minutes. Remove the pan from the heat and add the ketchup and dry spices. When mixture is cool use a blender or food processor to puree the sauce. Refrigerate in a covered container and prepare the ribs.

Preheat the oven to 300°F. Rinse the ribs, pat dry, and place them, bone side down, in a shallow 13 x 9 baking dish. In a small mixing bowl, combine the salt, pepper, chili powder, and brown sugar. Generously rub the ribs with this mixture. Place the ribs in the oven and cook, uncovered, for 1 to 1½ hours. Transfer to cutting board to cool for 10 minutes.

Preheat the grill to 300°F. Place the ribs on aluminum foil, bone side down. Smother with the prepared barbecue sauce. Place the ribs on the top rack of the grill or another indirect heat source. Grill for 20 minutes, or to the desired tenderness; the ribs should appear to be a rich golden brown. Let rest before serving and serve with barbecue sauce.

RIBS

2 racks baby back pork ribs

¼ cup sea salt

¼ cup freshly cracked black pepper

¼ cup chili powder

½ cup dark brown sugar, packed

Grilled Pork Tenderloin with Huckleberry Cream Sauce

Different cheeses will vary the flavor of this light cream sauce. Fontina is our favorite.

Serves 4

1 (1- to 2-pound) pork tenderloin

2 tablespoons olive oil

1 tablespoon sea salt

2 tablespoons pepper, divided

½ cup chicken broth

⅓ cup half-and-half

3 tablespoons fresh huckleberries

¼ cup soft cheese (such as blue, goat, or fontina)

Place the whole pork tenderloin between sheets of waxed paper. Tenderize the pork to about 2 inches by pounding with a meat mallet until somewhat flat. Then place the tenderloin in a shallow baking dish and rub with the olive oil, salt, and half the pepper. Let rest for at least 10 minutes at room temperature.

Heat a small saucepan over medium-low heat. Whisk in the chicken broth and the half-and-half, then add huckleberries. Let it simmer 5 minutes, until the sauce is silky in texture. Remove from the heat. Immediately add the cheese and remaining black pepper to taste.

Preheat a grill to 400°F. Grill the tenderloin on each side for 10 minutes, or to the desired doneness. Remove it from the grill and let rest to allow the juices to redistribute. Slice the pork and transfer it to a serving platter. Drizzle with cream sauce.

Panfried Trout with Huckleberry Lemon Sauce

This is a regional dish, through and through, with regional ingredients. The epitome for ultimate freshness is to catch your own trout and pick your own berries.

Serves 4

To prepare sauce, combine all sauce ingredients in a blender and blend until everything is incorporated. Set aside and prepare the fish.

Combine the dry ingredients (flour through dried oregano) in a large resealable plastic bag and shake until well mixed. Set aside.

In a shallow baking dish, combine the eggs and milk, mixing thoroughly. Dip the fish fillets in the egg mixture, coating both sides. One at a time, place the fillets in the plastic bag containing the dry breading mix and shake until well coated.

In a large frying pan, heat the oil. Transfer each fish fillet to the pan and cook until golden brown, about 5 minutes per side. Serve the sauce on top.

SAUCE

¼ cup fresh huckleberries

2 tablespoons fresh lemon juice

Salt and pepper

TROUT

2 cups all-purpose flour

½ cup cornmeal

2 tablespoons salt

2 tablespoons ground mustard

2 tablespoons smoked paprika

2 tablespoons granulated garlic

1 tablespoon black pepper

1 teaspoon cayenne pepper

½ teaspoon dried thyme

½ teaspoon dried oregano

2 large eggs

½ cup milk

4 trout fillets

½ cup vegetable oil

Roast Duck with Huckleberry Hoisin

Huckleberries provide the sweetness in this Chinese barbecue sauce that marries well with the duck.

Serves 2–4

1 (4- to 5-pound) duck

½ lemon

½ medium onion

Trim the excess fat from the duck. Rinse the duck thoroughly, inside and out, and pat dry with paper towels. Place one half a lemon and one half of onion in the cavity of the duck. Tie the legs together with kitchen twine. Place the duck in a large resealable plastic bag.

In a large mixing bowl, whisk together all the marinade ingredients. Pour the marinade into the plastic bag, seal, and shake, making sure the mixture is well distributed. Place the bagged duck in a roasting pan. Refrigerate for at least 4 hours or overnight, rotating every so often to redistribute the marinade.

Preheat the oven to 375°F. Remove the duck from the plastic bag (do not discard the marinade) and place it on a rack in the roasting pan, breast side up. Place pan on the center rack in the oven.

While duck is roasting, pour the marinade from the bag into a small saucepan and reduce it over medium-high heat by half for 15 minutes. Brush the reduced marinade over duck about every 20 minutes during the roasting process. If the skin begins to get too brown, tent foil over the duck. Cook for a total of about 2 hours; the internal temperature should reach 180°F. Let the duck sit 10 minutes before carving.

MARINADE

2 cups huckleberry wine

½ cup soy sauce

¼ cup rice vinegar

2 tablespoons huckleberry preserves

2 tablespoons hoisin sauce

2 tablespoons peeled and chopped fresh ginger

6 cloves garlic, peeled and smashed

½ medium onion, chopped

Juice of ½ lemon

2 tablespoons gochujang (Korean hot chili pepper paste)

1 teaspoon Chinese five-spice powder

1 teaspoon dry mustard

1 teaspoon freshly ground black pepper

Coq au Huckleberry Vin

Coq au vin, or "rooster with wine," is a classic French dish. Variations abound in France, as different areas utilize their own wines and champagnes. Here's our own regional adaptation of this rich and delicious dish.

Serves 8–10

3 tablespoons olive oil

½ pound thick-cut bacon, diced

1 chicken (about 3 pounds), rinsed and quartered

¾ cup coarsely chopped shallots

2 pounds carrots, peeled and cut into 1-inch lengths

3 tablespoons chopped garlic

3 tablespoons unsalted butter

2 pounds white mushrooms, cleaned and quartered

3 tablespoons all-purpose flour

2 cups chicken broth

2 cups huckleberry wine

1 tablespoon huckleberry preserves

¼ cup tomato paste

1 tablespoon fresh chopped thyme

1 bay leaf

Salt and pepper

6 tablespoons chopped fresh parsley

16 ounces egg noodles

Preheat the oven to 375 °F. In a large dutch oven, heat the oil over medium-high heat. Add the bacon and render (the cooking process of extracting the fat) until the bacon is brown and crispy. Transfer the cooked bacon, leaving the fat, to a paper-towel-lined bowl to drain.

Using the same dutch oven, brown the chicken in the bacon fat, about 5 minutes per side. Remove the chicken to drain and set aside.

Reduce the heat to medium-low. Add the shallots and carrots to the dutch oven and cook for about 10 minutes, until soft. Add the garlic and cook 4 more minutes. Next, add the butter and mushrooms and cook 6 minutes. Stir the flour into the vegetable mixture and let cook a few more minutes. (This makes the roux, or thickener, for the sauce.)

Deglaze the pan by adding the chicken broth and huckleberry wine, scraping the bottom to extract the flavor of any bits left in the pot. Next add the huckleberry preserves, tomato paste, thyme, bay leaf, and salt and pepper to taste.

Stir the drained bacon into the mixture and add chicken. Spoon the sauce mixture over the chicken until it is well coated. Bring everything to a boil. Immediately remove from the heat, cover pot, place it in oven, and cook for 35 minutes. Uncover and cook for another 30 minutes. Add the parsley and cook for a final 5 minutes. In the meantime, prepare egg noodles according to the package instructions.

Remove the pot from oven and serve the chicken, vegetables, and sauce over the cooked noodles.

Grilled Rib Eye with Huckleberry Caramelized Onions

When prepared, the caramelized onions turn a purplish-blue color, and they taste as good as they look.

Serves 4

1 tablespoon unsalted butter

1 teaspoon olive oil

2 cups medium thinly sliced sweet onions

Pinch of salt

½ teaspoon black pepper

½ cup fresh huckleberries

4 rib-eye steaks

Grilling spice of your choice

Prepare rib eye by rubbing in grilling spice on both sides of steaks, set aside.

Melt the butter and olive oil together in a large frying pan. Over medium heat, sauté the onions until translucent. Add salt and pepper, and cook for 1 minute. Add the huckleberries and cook until onions become caramelized (brown and crispy).

Meanwhile preheat the grill to 400°F. Cook the rib eyes to the desired doneness. Depends on cut and doneness preference. Serve the onions atop the steaks.

Huckleberry Barbecue Pulled Pork Sandwich with Broccoli Slaw

This sandwich and slaw combination makes for good old comfort food.

12–18 sandwiches

To prepare the pork, combine the dry ingredients in a small bowl. Place the pork in a roasting pan, rub it with the spice mixture, cover, and refrigerate overnight.

The next day, preheat the oven to 300°F. Roast the pork until it starts to fall apart, up to 6 hours; the internal temperature should be 165°F to 170°F. Take the roast out of the oven and let rest for about 15 minutes or until it is cool enough to handle. Shred by hand and set aside.

The pulled pork can be frozen or stored in the refrigerator for up to 3 to 5 days.

PULLED PORK

2 tablespoons smoked paprika

2 tablespoons salt

2 tablespoons dark brown sugar

1 tablespoon black pepper

1 tablespoon granulated garlic

1 tablespoon granulated onion

1 teaspoon dry mustard

1 (5-pound) pork butt

Store-bought buns or rolls (a substantial ciabatta is recommended)

Huckleberry Barbecue Sauce (see page 137)

To make the slaw, place the broccoli slaw mix into a large bowl. In a separate bowl, whisk together the mayonnaise, canola oil, sugar, vinegar, salt, and huckleberries. Blend thoroughly. Pour the dressing mixture over broccoli slaw mix and toss to coat. Cover and chill at least 2 hours before serving.

Assemble the sandwich by putting a bun on each plate. Place pulled pork on the bottom bun and top with huckleberry barbecue sauce. Spoon broccoli slaw on top of pulled pork, and add bun top. Enjoy y'all!

HUCKLEBERRY BROCCOLI SLAW

1 (8-ounce) bag broccoli slaw mix

⅓ cup mayonnaise

1 tablespoon plus 1 teaspoon canola oil

¼ cup sugar

1 tablespoon apple cider vinegar

⅛ teaspoon salt

3 tablespoons fresh or frozen huckleberries

Huckleberry Seafood Salad

This salad is equally good with crab, lobster, and shrimp—it's the huckleberries that make it special.

4–6 servings

¼ cup orange juice

¼ cup extra-virgin olive oil

1 tablespoon champagne vinegar or white wine vinegar

2 teaspoons finely chopped shallot

¼ teaspoon salt

Pinch of ground pepper

10 cups torn red leaf lettuce

¾ cup fresh huckleberries

¼ cup slivered red onion

1 tablespoon chopped fresh tarragon

1 pound chopped cooked lobster meat or crabmeat (about 2¾ cups) or small boiled shrimp

6 tablespoons toasted sliced almonds

In a blender combine the first six ingredients (orange juice through pepper). Blend until smooth.

In a large bowl, toss the lettuce, huckleberries, onion, and tarragon with half the vinaigrette. In another bowl, gently mix the seafood with the remaining vinaigrette. Combine the ingredients from both bowls and sprinkle the almonds on top. Alternatively, divide the lettuce mixture among six dinner plates and top with the seafood and almonds.

Desserts

Huckleberry Blueberry Cobbler

Quick and easy, this dish is particularly delicious when served with vanilla ice cream or freshly whipped cream. Mix berries as instructed below, or make this with just huckleberries.

Serves 6–8

FILLING

1 cup huckleberries

1 cup blueberries

1 teaspoon freshly grated lemon zest

1 tablespoon fresh lemon juice

⅓ cup sugar

1 teaspoon cornstarch

TOPPING

⅔ cup all-purpose flour

1 teaspoon baking powder

¾ teaspoon nutmeg

½ cup heavy cream

Preheat the oven to 400° F. Generously butter an 8-inch (1½-quart) glass pie plate. In a medium bowl, toss together the berries, lemon zest and juice, sugar, and cornstarch until well mixed. Transfer the filling to the prepared pie plate.

In a medium mixing bowl, combine the flour, baking powder, and nutmeg. Add the cream and stir until the mixture begins to form a dough, making sure not to overmix. Drop ¼-cup dollops of dough onto the berry mixture. Bake on center rack in oven for 25 minutes, or until topping is golden brown.

Huckleberry Crisp

Serve this warm à la mode.

Serves 6–8

Preheat the oven to 375°F. Generously butter a
13 x 9 x 2-inch baking pan.

In a medium mixing bowl, combine the flour, sugar,
and cinnamon. With a pastry cutter or your fingertips, work in the butter until the mixture resembles
coarse meal.

Arrange an even layer of huckleberries in the
prepared pan. Sprinkle the crumb mixture over the
berries. Bake about 20 minutes, or until the top is
browned and the juices are bubbling.

¾ cup all-purpose flour

½ cup sugar

½ teaspoon cinnamon

6 tablespoons (¾ stick)
unsalted butter, chilled and
cut into ½-inch cubes

5 cups huckleberries

Huckleberry Crumb Cake

This is a refreshing dessert served with ice cream but is also suitable for brunch. It's best served freshly baked.

Serves 8–12

3 cups all-purpose flour

1 cup plus 2 tablespoons sugar

2 teaspoons baking powder

¾ teaspoon baking soda

¾ teaspoon salt

¾ teaspoon ground cinnamon

¼ teaspoon nutmeg

¾ cup (1½ sticks) plus 2 tablespoons (¼ stick) unsalted butter, chilled and cut into ½-inch cubes

2 large eggs

1 cup sour cream

2 teaspoons vanilla extract

3 cups huckleberries

Preheat the oven to 375°F. Prepare a 13 x 9 x 2-inch baking pan with cooking spray or butter and flour. In a medium mixing bowl, combine the flour, 1 cup sugar, baking powder, baking soda, salt, cinnamon, and nutmeg. Mix well with a spoon or whisk. Add ¾ cup butter. Mix the ingredients with your fingertips until mixture resembles coarse meal.

Transfer 1½ cups of the flour mixture to a separate bowl for the crumb topping and add the remaining 2 tablespoons butter and remaining 2 tablespoons sugar. Blend with your fingertips to form clumps. Set aside.

In a small mixing bowl, whisk together the eggs, sour cream, and vanilla. Add to the remaining flour mixture. Mix until batter forms, making sure not to overmix. Fold in the huckleberries. Pour the batter into the prepared pan. Evenly sprinkle the crumb topping over the batter. Bake on the oven's center rack for 40 to 45 minutes, or until an inserted knife pulls out clean. Cool in pan.

Huckleberry Lemon Trifle

Trifles are labor intensive to prepare but well worth the trouble. Don't worry if you have leftovers; like good lasagna, trifles get better as they age.

Serves 8–12

POUND CAKE

2¾ cups all-purpose flour

1¾ cups sugar

2 teaspoons baking powder

1 teaspoon salt

4 large eggs

1 cup (2 sticks) unsalted butter, melted

1 teaspoon vanilla extract

¾ cup milk

Tip: Simplify the preparation process by using a prepared pound cake.

Preheat the oven to 375°F. Prepare a 9 x 5-inch loaf pan with cooking spray or butter and flour. In a medium mixing bowl, combine the flour, sugar, baking powder, and salt. In a separate bowl, whisk the eggs and then add the butter, vanilla, and milk. Add the wet ingredients to the dry ingredients and mix completely. Pour the batter into the prepared pan and bake on the center rack in the oven for 1 hour to 1 hour and 10 minutes, or until an inserted knife pulls out clean. Cool completely, remove from pan, and cut into 2-inch cubes.

In a small saucepan combine all sauce ingredients, setting aside a handful of berries for garnish. Simmer over low heat, stirring occasionally, for 40 to 45 minutes; the sauce should reduce to about 2½ cups. Remove the pan from the heat and cool completely, transfer the sauce to a covered container and chill. The sauce may be made up to 2 days ahead.

To prepare lemon mousse, whisk together the egg yolks and sugar in a heavy saucepan. Add the lemon juice and butter. Cook over moderately low heat, whisking constantly, until the butter is completely melted. Continue to cook for approximately 10 more minutes, whisking constantly, until the mixture just reaches the boiling point and is thickened. Stir in the zest and let cool. Transfer the mousse to a mixing bowl, cover the surface of mixture with plastic wrap, and chill for about 2 hours.

Pour the cream into a medium mixing bowl. Using an electric mixer, beat the cream until stiff peaks form. Whisk approximately one-quarter of the whipped cream into the cooled lemon mixture. Gently fold in the remaining whipped cream, making sure not to overmix. Cover and chill. The mousse may be made up to 2 days ahead.

To assemble the trifle, arrange a layer of pound cake cubes on the bottom of a trifle dish. Spoon ½ cup of huckleberry sauce over the cubes. Next, spoon ¼ cup of lemon mousse over the sauce layer. Repeat this layering, ending with a mousse layer on top. Carefully cover the dish with plastic wrap and chill for several hours or preferably overnight. Before serving, garnish the top of trifle with more lemon zest and the reserved fresh berries.

HUCKLEBERRY SAUCE

5 cups frozen or fresh huckleberries

¾ cup sugar

½ cup water

1 tablespoon fresh lemon juice

LEMON MOUSSE

8 large egg yolks

1 cup sugar

¾ cup fresh lemon juice (about 3 large lemons)

7 tablespoons (⅞ stick) unsalted butter cut into ½-inch pieces, room temperature

1 tablespoon freshly grated lemon zest, plus more for garnish

1 cup heavy cream

Huckleberry Swirl Cheesecake Bars

Separately, shortbread and cheesecake are rich. Together, they form an intoxicating indulgence. Add huckleberries to that combination and you have something absolutely heavenly.

Makes 24 bars, approximately 2" x 2"

Preheat the oven to 350°F. In a food processor, combine the butter, flour, brown sugar, and salt. Process until mixture begins to take shape, forming small lumps. Gently press the mixture into the bottom of a 13 x 9 x 2-inch baking pan until evenly covered. Bake on the center rack for 20 minutes, or until golden. Remove the pan to a wire rack to cool completely; do not turn off the oven. While the crust bakes, prepare the cream cheese topping.

In a mixing bowl beat the cream cheese with an electric mixer until smooth, about 1 minute. Beat in the eggs, one at a time. Add the granulated sugar and vanilla. Remove one-third of the cream cheese mixture and incorporate huckleberry preserves. Pour the plain cream cheese mixture evenly onto the cooled crust. Spoon dollops of huckleberry cream cheese mixture onto the plain cream cheese mixture. Use a knife to swirl the plain and huckleberry mixtures together. Bake on the center rack for 30 minutes or just before the tops start to brown. Cool completely in the pan and cut into 24 bars. Cover and refrigerate to store.

SHORTBREAD CRUST

¾ cup (1½ sticks) unsalted butter, chilled and cut into ½-inch pieces

2 cups all-purpose flour

½ cup packed brown sugar

½ teaspoon salt

CREAM CHEESE TOPPING

2 (8-ounce) packages cream cheese, room temperature

2 large eggs

¾ cup granulated sugar

1 teaspoon vanilla extract

¼ cup huckleberry preserves

Huckleberry Cupcakes with Lemon Cream Cheese Frosting

Not a berry muffin, these are truly cupcakes. Sweet and light, they are a nice variation of the popular white cupcake.

Makes 12 cupcakes

CUPCAKES

5 tablespoons unsalted butter, room temperature

1 cup granulated sugar

2 large eggs

1 teaspoon vanilla extract

2 cups all-purpose flour

1 tablespoon baking powder

¼ teaspoon salt

1 cup whole milk

1 cup frozen huckleberries

Tip: Using frozen berries will keep the huckleberries from sinking to the bottom of the cupcakes as they bake.

Preheat the oven to 350°F. Prepare 12 muffin tins with paper liners. In a large mixing bowl, place the butter and granulated sugar. Beat with an electric mixer for a few minutes until light and fluffy. Add the eggs and vanilla. Beat until well mixed.

In a separate bowl, sift together the flour, baking powder, and salt. Gradually add the dry ingredients to the butter mixture at low speed, alternating with the milk, beginning and ending with the flour mixture. Do not overmix. Fold in huckleberries.

Fill the prepared muffin cups about two-thirds full. Bake on the center rack in the oven 20 to 25 minutes, or until the tops are a pale golden color and an inserted knife or toothpick pulls out clean. Remove the cupcakes from the oven and place them on a wire rack to cool completely.

To prepare the frosting, combine the cream cheese, butter, vanilla, zest, and juice in a medium mixing bowl. Beat the ingredients with an electric mixer until light and fluffy. Gradually beat in the confectioners' sugar. Cover and refrigerate. Once cupcakes are cool and the frosting is firm, frost the cupcakes.

FROSTING

1 (8-ounce) package cream cheese, room temperature

2 tablespoons (¼ stick) unsalted butter, room temperature

½ teaspoon vanilla extract

¼ teaspoon freshly grated lemon zest

½ teaspoon lemon juice

½ cup confectioners' sugar

Huckleberry Pie with Lattice Crust

Serve this with plain vanilla or Huckleberry Ice Cream (see page 95). Simply perfection.

Serves 8

CRUST

2 cups all-purpose flour, plus more for rolling

½ teaspoon salt

12 tablespoons (1½ sticks) unsalted butter, chilled and cut into ½-inch cubes

3 tablespoons vegetable shortening, chilled and cut into ½-inch cubes

¼ cup ice water

PIE FILLING

4½ cups (2 pints) huckleberries

¾ cup sugar

¼ cup all-purpose flour

2 teaspoons freshly grated lemon zest

2 tablespoons lemon juice

1 teaspoon vanilla extract

In a large mixing bowl, combine the flour and salt. Add the butter and shortening. Using a pastry cutter or your fingertips, work them into the flour until the mixture resembles coarse meal. Very gradually add the ice water, bit by bit, working the dough as little as necessary and adding as little water as possible, until the pastry forms a ball. Divide dough in half and wrap in plastic and chill for at least 1 hour.

When ready to assemble the pie, place the oven rack in the lower third of the oven and preheat it to 400°F. Combine all filling ingredients in large bowl and mix thoroughly. Let stand for about 15 minutes. Prepare the egg wash by whisking the egg and cream together.

Transfer half of the dough onto a lightly floured work surface. Roll it out to a 12½-inch round. Brush it with the egg wash and place it in 9-inch pie dish, egg-wash side down. Pour the huckleberry filling into the crust. Roll out the second pie crust on a lightly floured surface to a 12-inch round. Cut the dough into generous ½-inch-wide strips. Arrange half the dough strips horizontally across the top of the filling, spacing them evenly apart (see picture). Form a lattice by weaving the remaining strips

EGG WASH

1 large egg

½ cup heavy cream

vertically. Trim the dough strips even with the overhang on the bottom crust. Press the dough strips and overhang together to seal and crimp the edges. Brush the crust with egg wash.

Place the pie on baking sheet to catch any over-flow. Bake for about 50 minutes, or until pie filling bubbles thickly in the center. Cool completely before serving.

Huckleberry Sorbet

Summer in a bowl—this sorbet is a refreshing dairy-free treat.

Makes about 4 cups

Place all the ingredients into a blender. Blend until smooth. Pour the mixture through a fine-mesh wire strainer placed over a bowl. Place in refrigerator to strain and cool, about 3 hours.

Once cooled and strained, pour the strained mixture from the bowl into an ice-cream machine and process according to the manufacturer's instructions. Transfer to an airtight container and freeze until ready to serve.

4 cups fresh or thawed huckleberries

2 cups sugar

2 cups water

3 tablespoons lemon juice

Bears and Huckleberries

In the Northern Rockies, huckleberries constitute an important source of food for grizzlies and black bears. The ripening of the huckleberries coincides with the final feeding stage before the bear's hibernation. Constituting approximately 15 percent of the bear's annual intake, huckleberries are a crucial nutritional element of their diet.

In the West, almost everyone has heard a story about a berry picker stumbling upon a bear. If you find yourself face-to-face with a bear while picking berries, even if you've found the mother lode, it behooves you not to compete with the bear. The bear won't share, so for your safety it's best to back away. There is no evidence that berriers run into bears more frequently than anyone else. Bears are normally shy, and if you stay in groups and make some noise while you are picking, bears are likely to stay away.

There is a precarious balance between people and bears, especially—perhaps—when it comes to huckleberries. Fortunately, however, bears tend to stick to the higher elevations for their berries, while humans tend to stay lower. This helps to maintain the balance.

Huckleberry Ice Cream

This easy no-cook ice cream is filled with purple gems.

Makes about 4 cups

Place the huckleberries, sugar, salt, and milk in a blender. Blend until smooth. Stir in the cream. Pour the mixture through a fine-mesh wire strainer placed over a bowl. Place in refrigerator to strain and cool, about 3 hours.

Pour the mixture into an ice-cream machine and process according to the manufacturer's instructions. Transfer to an airtight container and freeze until ready to serve.

2 cups fresh or thawed huckleberries

¾ cup sugar

⅛ teaspoon salt

1 cup milk

1½ cups heavy cream

Huckleberry Bundt Cake

The addition of huckleberries to this basic bundt cake enhances this classic favorite.

Serves 10–12

3 cups all-purpose flour

1 tablespoon baking powder

1 teaspoon salt

1⅔ cups granulated sugar

¾ cup (1½ sticks) unsalted butter, room temperature

3 large eggs

2 teaspoons vanilla extract

1 cup buttermilk

1½ cups frozen huckleberries

Huckleberry Glaze
(see page 135)

Confectioners' sugar

Tip: Using frozen berries will keep the huckleberries from sinking to the bottom of the cake as it bakes.

Preheat the oven to 350°F. Prepare a 10-inch-diameter bundt pan with cooking spray or butter and flour. In a medium bowl, whisk together the flour, baking powder, and salt. Using an electric mixer, beat the granulated sugar and butter in a separate bowl until light and fluffy. Beat in the eggs and vanilla. Add the dry ingredients in batches, alternating with the buttermilk. Fold in huckleberries.

Pour the batter into prepared pan. Bake on the center rack in the oven for 50 to 60 minutes, or until an inserted knife pulls out clean. Remove the pan from oven and let the cake cool completely in the pan. Transfer the cake from the bundt pan to a serving plate, pour huckleberry glaze over cake, and dust with confectioners' sugar.

Chocolate Torte with Huckleberry Filling and Ganache

True chocoholics and huckleberry lovers alike will relish in this rich, dense, and decadent dessert.

Serves 12–16

Preheat the oven to 325°F. Prepare a 9½-inch springform pan with cooking spray or butter and flour.

In a large saucepan combine the semisweet chocolate, butter, and granulated sugar. Cook over moderate heat until the chocolate and butter have melted and the sugar has dissolved. Remove from the heat and stir in the vanilla. Let stand for 10 minutes.

Once the chocolate mixture is cool, whisk the egg yolks into the chocolate mixture, one at a time, beating well after each addition. Stir in the flour.

In a separate large bowl, beat the egg whites until foamy. Add the cream of tartar and salt. Beat until stiff peaks form. Whisk one-third of the egg whites into the chocolate mixture. Carefully fold in the remaining whites. Pour the batter into prepared pan. Bake on the center rack in the oven for 45 to 60 minutes, or until an inserted knife pulls out clean. Remove the pan from oven and transfer to a wire cooling rack. Carefully remove the sides of

CAKE

1 (8-ounce) package semisweet chocolate, broken into squares

¾ cup (1½ sticks) unsalted butter, cut into ½-inch cubes

½ cup granulated sugar

2 teaspoons vanilla extract

5 eggs, separated

¼ cup all-purpose flour

Dash of cream of tartar

Dash of salt

Tip: For the filling, store-bought preserves can substitute for the homemade huckleberry jam.

the springform pan once cooled and then gently remove the base.

To prepare the ganache, heat the cream and butter in a heavy saucepan over medium heat. Bring it just to a boil. Remove from the heat and whisk in the chocolate. Let cool, stirring occasionally, until chocolate is completely melted and the ganache has thickened but still pourable.

To assemble, carefully cut the cake in half horizontally. Cover the bottom cake layer with huckleberry jam and replace the top layer. Pour the ganache over cake. Use a rubber spatula to smooth the ganache over the top and sides until evenly coated. Let stand about 1 hour before serving. Dust with confectioners' sugar for a polished presentation.

GANACHE

¾ cup heavy cream

2 tablespoons (¼ stick) unsalted butter

1 (8-ounce) package bittersweet chocolate, chopped

FILLING

1 cup Huckleberry Jam (see page 134)

Confectioners' sugar, for dusting

Vanilla Bean Cheesecake with Huckleberry Glaze

This classic cheesecake is enhanced by fresh vanilla and huckleberries.

Serves 8–12

CRUST

2⅓ cups graham cracker crumbs

½ cup (1 stick) unsalted butter, melted

¼ cup sugar

CHEESECAKE

2 vanilla beans, split lengthwise

⅓ cup heavy cream

3 (8-ounce) packages cream cheese, room temperature

1 cup sugar

½ cup sour cream

2 teaspoons vanilla extract

4 large eggs

TOPPING

Huckleberry Glaze
(see page 135)

Preheat the oven to 375°F. Wrap the outside of a 10-inch-diameter springform pan with aluminum foil.

In a bowl combine all crust ingredients. Using a pastry cutter, your fingertips, or a food processor, blend until moist crumbs form. Press the mixture firmly onto the bottom and the sides of the prepared pan to form pie crust. Bake on the center rack in the oven for 10 minutes, or until the crust begins to brown. Transfer the pan to a rack and let cool. Maintain the oven temperature while preparing cheesecake filling.

Scrape the seeds from the split vanilla beans into a heavy saucepan set over medium heat. Add the beans and the cream, stir and bring the mixture to a boil. Immediately remove the pan from the heat and let the mixture cool completely. Strain the mixture through a fine-mesh wire strainer and discard the vanilla beans. Set aside.

Using an electric mixer, beat the cream cheese and sugar in large bowl for several minutes until smooth. Add the vanilla-cream mixture, sour cream, and vanilla extract. Beat until well blended. Beat in the eggs until thoroughly incorporated. Pour the filling into the prepared crust and bake for about 1 hour. The cheesecake should be golden and beginning to crack around the edges. Cool completely and remove from the pan. Top with huckleberry glaze.

Huckleberry Crème Brûlée

A kitchen torch is required for this recipe, so proceed with caution. Trust us; it's worth it. This recipe can be doubled or tripled.

Serves 2–3, depending on ramekin size

1 cup heavy cream, chilled

2 tablespoons plus 1 teaspoon granulated sugar

Pinch of table salt

3 large egg yolks

½ teaspoon vanilla extract

½ teaspoon grated orange zest

¼ cup huckleberries

2–4 teaspoons turbinado sugar

Adjust the oven rack to the lower third of the oven and preheat the oven to 300°F.

Combine ½ cup cream, granulated sugar, and salt in small saucepan; bring the mixture to a boil over medium heat, stirring occasionally to ensure that the sugar dissolves. Remove from the heat to cool.

Meanwhile, place a kitchen towel in the bottom of a baking dish or roasting pan and arrange two or three 4- to 5-ounce ramekins (or shallow fluted dishes) on the towel. Bring a kettle of water to a boil over high heat.

After the cream-sugar mixture has cooled slightly, stir in the remaining ½ cup cream to cool the mixture further. In a medium bowl, whisk the yolks until broken up and combined. Whisk the vanilla, orange zest, and about ¼ cup of the cream mixture into the yolks until loosened and combined; repeat with another ¼ cup cream mixture. Add the remaining cream mixture and whisk until evenly colored and thoroughly combined. Strain through fine-mesh wire strainer into a 2-cup measuring cup or pitcher (or clean bowl); discard the solids in the strainer. Gently Add ¼ cup huckleberries to the

mixture. Pour or ladle the mixture into the ramekins, dividing it evenly among them.

Carefully place the baking dish and ramekins on the oven rack; pour boiling water into baking dish, taking care not to splash water into ramekins, until the water reaches two-thirds the height of the ramekins. Bake until the centers of the custards are just barely set and are no longer sloshy and a digital instant-read thermometer inserted in the centers registers 170°F to 175°F, 35 to 40 minutes (30 to 35 minutes for shallow fluted dishes). Begin checking the temperature about 5 minutes before the recommended time.

Transfer the ramekins from baking dish to a wire rack; cool to room temperature, about 2 hours. Cover each ramekin tightly with plastic wrap and refrigerate until cold, at least 4 hours and up to 4 days.

TO SERVE

Uncover the ramekins; if condensation has collected on the custards, gently place a paper towel on the surface to soak up the moisture. Sprinkle each with about 1 to 1½ teaspoons of turbinado sugar; tilt and tap each ramekin for even coverage. Ignite the torch and caramelize the sugar until tops are golden in color. Refrigerate the ramekins, uncovered, to re-chill the custard, 30 to 45 minutes (but no longer). Serve and enjoy.

Choco-Huck Party Cupcakes

Using a mix makes this an easy party recipe!

Makes 18–20 cupcakes

For the cake, preheat the oven to 350°F. Prepare the chocolate cake mix according to the instructions on the box. Set the batter aside.

In a large bowl, beat the cream cheese with a mixer until smooth. Add the egg and beat until well mixed. Beat in the sugar and salt. Fold in the huckleberries and chocolate chips, if using.

Line muffin tins with cupcake liners. Spoon the chocolate batter into the muffin cups until it fills approximately one-third of each. Drop a tablespoon of cream cheese filling on top of batter in each muffin cup, then cover the filling with more chocolate batter until muffin cup is ⅔ full.

Bake for 16 minutes, or until a toothpick inserted in the center of the cupcake comes out clean. Cool completely.

CAKE

1 chocolate cake mix (and the ingredients listed on the box for preparation)

1 (8-ounce) package cream cheese, room temperature

1 large egg

½ cup sugar

¼ teaspoon salt

1 cup fresh huckleberries plus ¼ cup huckleberries to decorate cupcakes

1 cup mini chocolate chips (optional)

For the buttercream frosting, place all ingredients in a deep mixing bowl, starting with lower amounts of vanilla and milk; increase them as needed for taste preference and consistency. Start mixing with an electric mixer on low speed to prevent the confectioners' sugar from flying around and making a mess. When combined, increase the speed to medium and beat until frosting is smooth and spreadable.

Frost the cupcakes and decorate with chocolate sprinkles and fresh huckleberries.

BUTTERCREAM FROSTING

4 cups confectioners' sugar

1 cup (2 sticks) butter (salted or unsalted—your choice), room temperature

1–2 teaspoons vanilla extract

1–2 tablespoons milk

chocolate sprinkles

Huckleberry Tartufos with Salted Caramel Sauce

Tartufo is an Italian ice-cream dessert typically made with fruit flavors such as cherries or strawberries. We think huckleberries make for the perfect tartufo.

Serves 4

SALTED CARAMEL SAUCE

1 cup sugar

¼ cup water

¾ cup heavy cream

3½ tablespoons unsalted butter

1 teaspoon salt

TARTUFOS

¾ cup crushed chocolate cookies

½ cup finely chopped bittersweet chocolate

1 pint vanilla ice cream

⅓ cup huckleberries

Fresh mint leaves, for garnish

SALTED CARAMEL SAUCE

In a medium-sized heavy saucepan, combine the sugar and water over medium-low heat and stir until the sugar dissolves. Increase the heat and bring to a boil without stirring. If necessary, use a wet pastry brush to wash down any crystals on the side of the pan. Boil until the syrup is a deep amber color, 5 to 6 minutes.

Remove the saucepan from the heat and carefully whisk in the heavy cream. The mixture will bubble. Stir in the unsalted butter and salt until the butter melts. Transfer the caramel to a heatproof dish and let cool.

The salted caramel sauce will keep up to 2 weeks refrigerated in a covered container. Reheat before serving, if desired.

TARTUFOS

Combine the cookie crumbs and chocolate in a large resealable bag.

Place the ice cream in a bowl and allow it to soften enough to gently mix in the huckleberries. Place

the ice cream back in the freezer for 1½ hours or longer, until the ice cream re-hardens.

Using a 4-ounce ice cream scoop, remove out a ball of ice cream. Place the remaining ice cream back in the freezer. Working quickly, put the ball of ice cream into the bag of cookie and chocolate pieces. Shake it around, pressing gently to completely coat the ice cream. Put the coated ice cream ball on a tray and freeze for 30 minutes. Repeat the process with the remaining ice cream.

TO SERVE

Drizzle warm or cold caramel sauce onto four dessert plates. Remove the tartufos from the freezer and cut a slice to show the inside of the ice cream ball. Arrange the tartufos on the plates with a drizzle or more of caramel and garnish with mint leaves.

Huckleberry Capital of the World

In 1981, the Montana State Legislature officially proclaimed Trout Creek, Montana, the "Huckleberry Capital of the World." A small town in the northwestern part of the state, Trout Creek is famous for its abundance of the purple berry and is home to the premier huckleberry festival in the West. During the second week in August, visitors from near and far flock to the town to eat and celebrate the juicy berry that embodies the spirit of the region. Festival activities include a 5K run, a huckleberry pancake breakfast, a parade, and the grand huckleberry festival auction, to name just a few. The weekend's activities culminate in arguably everyone's favorite event—the huckleberry dessert contest.

Huckleberry Thumbprint Cookies

Filled with oats, carrots, and raisins, these healthy cookies are just right with a dollop of huckleberry jam.

Makes 1½ dozen

½ cup (1 stick) unsalted butter, melted,

½ cup packed light brown sugar

½ cup granulated sugar

1 large egg yolk, room temperature

1 cup all-purpose flour

½ teaspoon ground ginger

½ teaspoon ground cinnamon

¾ teaspoon coarse salt

¾ cup old-fashioned rolled oats

¾ cup packed finely grated carrots (from about 3)

¼ cup chopped golden raisins

¾ cup finely chopped pecans

¼ cup (½ stick) unsalted butter, room temperature

¼ cup confectioners' sugar

2 ounces cream cheese, room temperature

2–3 teaspoons huckleberry jam

Preheat the oven to 350°F and line baking sheets with parchment paper. In a large bowl, whisk together the melted butter, both sugars, and egg yolk. In another bowl, whisk together the flour, ginger, cinnamon, and salt. Stir the flour mixture into the butter mixture to combine. Mix in the oats, carrots, and raisins. Cover and refrigerate 30 minutes.

Roll the dough into 1½-inch balls (about 1 tablespoon); roll balls in chopped pecans to coat. Set them 2 inches apart on parchment-lined baking sheets. Bake 10 minutes. Remove from oven; press an indentation into the center of each cookie with the end of a wooden spoon. Bake cookies until golden brown on the bottom, 10 to 12 minutes more. Transfer cookies to a wire rack; let cool.

In a bowl, beat the remaining ¼ cup butter and confectioners' sugar on slow, gradually building to medium speed, until smooth. Beat in the cream cheese until just combined. Swirl in jam. Fill the center of each cookie with cream-cheese mixture before serving.

Hucks 'n' Cream Frozen Pops

These pops are a cool treat on a hot day—or a great snack no matter the weather.

Makes 4–6 pops, depending on the size of your molds

In a blender combine the huckleberries, sugar, and lemon juice. Blend until the mixture is finely pureed. Transfer the puree to a bowl.

Place the cream in a medium bowl and beat with an electric mixer until soft peaks form. Add the vanilla and beat again just enough to incorporate the vanilla.

Gently pour the whipped cream on top of the huckleberry puree and, with just a few strokes, fold the cream into the puree to form streaks. You don't want the cream to combine with the puree; you want the two to remain as separate as possible. Spoon the mixture into ice-pop molds leaving a ½-inch gap at the top, and freeze them solid before serving (about 2 hours). If you don't have molds, freeze the mixture in small paper cups and insert a plastic spoon for a handle.

1⅓ cups fresh huckleberries

¼ cup sugar

1–2 tablespoons fresh lemon juice, or to taste

¾ cup heavy cream

1 teaspoon vanilla extract

Drinks

Huckleberry Banana Smoothie

For an even healthier and protein-packed drink, add a serving of whey protein powder, 1 tablespoon flaxseed oil, and substitute soy milk for cow's milk.

Makes 1 large smoothie

1 banana, ripe

¾ cup huckleberries

¼ cup vanilla yogurt

¾ cup milk

½ cup crushed ice

Dash of cinnamon

Combine all ingredients in a blender and puree until smooth.

Huckleberry Margarita on the Rocks

A recipe for the margarita lover looking for a new twist.

Makes 2 drinks

Rub the rim of two rocks or margarita glasses with a lime wedge. Swirl the rims through a small pile of salt to coat them. Add ice cubes to the glasses.

In a cocktail shaker, muddle the huckleberries and lime juice until the berries are pulverized. Add the tequila, simple syrup, bitters, and a handful of ice to the shaker. Add a leftover wedge or two from the limes. Shake vigorously for 15 seconds, and then strain into the salted glasses.

1 lime, cut into wedges

Kosher or sea salt, for rimming the glasses

Ice cubes

¼ cup fresh huckleberries

⅓ cup lime juice

½ cup tequila

1 tablespoon Huckleberry Simple Syrup (see page 146)

Dash of bitters

Huckleberry Frozen Margaritas

This is a frosty summer treat with a swirl of huckleberry.

Makes 4 drinks

1 lime, cut into wedges

Kosher or sea salt, for rimming the glasses

About 40 ounces (5 cups) ice cubes*

6 ounces frozen limeade concentrate

3 ounces frozen orange juice concentrate

¾ cup tequila

½ cup triple sec

4 teaspoons Huckleberry Coulis, divided (see page 132)

*Add additional ice to reach desired thickness

To salt the rims of margarita glasses, rub each rim with a cut lime slice and press the rim into a plate of salt.

Combine all the remaining ingredients except the huckleberry coulis in a blender and blend until smooth. Pour into glasses and swirl 1 teaspoon huckleberry coulis into each drink.

Huckleberry Lemon Frappe

This is an incredibly frothy, light, and incredibly satisfying fruit slushy.

Makes 4 (10-ounce) frappes

Combine all huckleberry sauce ingredients in a small heavy saucepan. Simmer on moderately low heat, stirring occasionally, for about 10 minutes. Cool completely. Sauce is best made ahead so it is cold for assembly. Store in refrigerator up to 1 week.

Just before serving, make the lemon slush by placing frozen lemonade, limoncello, and 1 drop yellow food coloring, if using, in a blender and blend to a slushy consistency.

ASSEMBLE THE FRAPPE

Place a heaping tablespoon of softened vanilla ice cream in the bottom of a 10-ounce glass. Top with 1 tablespoon huckleberry sauce. Top with one-fourth of the lemon slush. Top with one-fourth of remaining ice cream. Garnish with a few huckleberries. Repeat with the remaining three glasses and serve immediately.

HUCKLEBERRY SAUCE

½ cup huckleberries

1 tablespoon sugar

½ teaspoon lemon juice

½ teaspoon vanilla extract

LEMON SLUSH

2 cups lemonade (your favorite), frozen

4 tablespoons limoncello

Yellow food coloring (optional)

3 cups premium vanilla ice cream, softened

Fresh huckleberries, for garnish

Huckleberry Lemonade

Refreshing, tart, and sweet—this is a refreshing drink when you need one.

Makes 1 quart

½ cup lemon juice

½ cup sugar or Huckleberry Simple Syrup (see page 146)

3¼ cups water

½ cup fresh or thawed huckleberries

1 lemon, sliced

1 lime, sliced

Ice cubes

Frozen huckleberries, for serving

Combine the lemon juice, sugar, water, and huckleberries in a blender or food processor and puree. Pour the mixture into a quart-size pitcher or container.

Add the lemon and lime slices and stir. Add as much ice as you desire, cover, and refrigerate for at least 1 hour before serving.

Add a lemon and lime slice and a few whole frozen huckleberries to each glass when serving for a pop of color and as a way to keep the lemonade cooler for longer.

Tip: For a very refreshing beverage, fill the glass one-half to two-thirds full with Huckleberry Lemonade and top off with sparkling water or club soda.

Huckleberry Mojitos

Here are a couple of good recipes for the Cuban cocktail that depart from tradition—your preference.

HUCKLEBERRY RUM MOJITO

Makes 1 drink

½ lime

10 fresh mint leaves

1 tablespoon fresh huckleberries

3 ounces rum

1½ ounces triple sec

1–2 tablespoons Huckleberry Simple Syrup (see page 146), to taste

Ice cubes

Club soda

Squeeze the lime juice into a tall glass. Cut the lime half into 3 wedges and drop them in the glass. Muddle together the lime juice and wedges, mint, and huckleberries. Stir in the rum, triple sec, and simple syrup. Fill the glass with ice cubes and top it off with club soda. Stir and enjoy.

HUCKLEBERRY VODKA MOJITO

Makes 1 drink

¼ cup fresh huckleberries

6 fresh mint leaves, torn

Ice cubes

1½ ounces vodka

2 tablespoons fresh lime juice

1 tablespoon Huckleberry Simple Syrup (see recipe page 146)

Splash of tonic water or carbonated beverage of choice

Fresh huckleberries, for garnish

Fresh mint leaves, for garnish

Muddle the huckleberries and torn mint leaves in a tall glass. Fill the glass halfway with ice cubes and stir in vodka, lime juice, and simple syrup. Top the glass with tonic. Stir well and garnish with fresh huckleberries and mint.

Huckleberry Lemon Drop

A refreshing summer martini to please your taste buds.

Makes 1 drink

1 lemon wedge

Superfine sugar, for the glass rim (optional)

1½ ounces vodka

½ ounce limoncello liqueur

½ ounce fresh lemon juice

¼ ounce Huckleberry Simple Syrup (see page 146)

Ice cubes

Lemon twist, for garnish (optional)

Coat the edge of the martini glass with the lemon wedge. Dip the edge of the glass in superfine sugar, if desired. Combine the remaining ingredients (except the lemon twist) in a cocktail shaker and shake vigorously. Pour the mixture into the prepared glass and serve with a lemon twist, if desired.

Staples

Huckleberry Coulis

Drizzle this sauce over cheesecake, ice cream, waffles, pancakes, or any dish needing some extra pizzazz. This is also our basic syrup recipe that can be used for pancakes, fruit salad, or any other dish that needs a little huckleberry drizzle or as a basic substitute for syrup.

Makes about 1½ cups

1½ cups fresh huckleberries

¼ cup sugar

1 teaspoon lemon juice

1 teaspoon vanilla or almond extract

Place the huckleberries in blender or food processor and puree. In a heavy saucepan combine the puree, sugar, lemon juice, and extract. Simmer over moderately low heat, stirring occasionally, for about 10 minutes. Remove from the heat and strain through a fine-mesh wire sieve; discard the solids in the sieve. Transfer the mixture to a bowl or squeeze bottle and chill until completely cooled before serving. (*Note:* Can add water as needed for desired consistency.)

Huckleberry Compote

More substantial than a coulis or glaze, compote is less of an accent and more of a hearty topping.

Makes about 2 cups

In heavy saucepan combine 1½ cups berries, sugar, water, and spices. Simmer over medium heat until the berries burst, stirring often, about 10 minutes. Add the remaining 1 cup berries. Continue stirring and cook until the mixture coats the back of a spoon, about 10 minutes. until all the berries have burst. Serve warm. This can be stored and reheated.

2½ cups huckleberries, divided

⅓ cup sugar

⅓ cup water

1 teaspoon ground cinnamon

1 teaspoon ground cloves

1 teaspoon ground or grated nutmeg

Huckleberry Jam

This freezer jam is quick and easy to prepare and delicious on fresh bread.

Makes 7 cups (3½ pints)

4½ cups fresh crushed huckleberries

5 cups sugar

6 ounces liquid fruit pectin

2 tablespoons lemon juice

In a large bowl, combine the crushed berries and sugar. Mix thoroughly. Let stand for 10 minutes. Add liquid pectin and lemon juice. Stir continuously for 3 minutes. Pour the jam into freezer containers, leaving a ½-inch gap at the top for expansion. Place the containers in the refrigerator and let stand until the jam sets, about 3 hours. Serve or transfer to the freezer. Fresh jam can be refrigerated up to 3 weeks.

Huckleberry Glaze

A wonderful garnish for desserts, this glaze can also be applied to baked ham.

Makes 2 cups

In a heavy saucepan, combine all ingredients. Over medium heat bring the mixture to a boil. Stir continuously for 1 minute. Remove from heat and cool slightly. Store in refrigerator up to 1 week.

2 cups fresh huckleberries

½ cup water

1 tablespoon sugar

2 teaspoons cornstarch

Huckleberry Vinaigrette

This vinaigrette makes any salad special.

Makes 1½ cups

¼ cup huckleberry vinegar

½ cup olive oil

2 tablespoons huckleberry preserves

¾ cup chopped walnuts

½ teaspoon salt

¼ teaspoon freshly ground black pepper

Tip: Huckleberry vinegar can be hard to find. If necessary, substitute red wine vinegar for it in this recipe.

In a small mixing bowl, whisk together the vinegar, oil, and huckleberry preserves. Add walnuts, salt, and pepper. Whisk dressing until well blended. Store in fridge up to 1 week.

Huckleberry Barbecue Sauce

From fish to foul, try this sauce on anything that needs an extra kick.

Makes about 3 cups

In medium saucepan, combine the tomatoes, tomato paste, vinegars, and Worcestershire sauce. Bring to a boil over medium high heat. Reduce the heat and simmer 15 minutes. Add the remaining ingredients, stir, and simmer another 15 minutes. Set aside to cool. Use blender or food processor to puree the sauce. Store in refrigerator up to one week.

2 (14½-ounce) cans diced tomatoes

1 tablespoon tomato paste

1 tablespoon apple cider vinegar

1 teaspoon balsamic vinegar

2 teaspoons Worcestershire sauce

1 tablespoon molasses

½ cup brown sugar packed

3 tablespoons huckleberry preserves

1 jalapeño pepper, seeded and chopped

½ bell pepper

4 cloves garlic, peeled and chopped

1 teaspoon granulated onion

1 teaspoon dry mustard

1 teaspoon freshly ground black pepper

1 teaspoon sea salt

Pinch of crushed red pepper (optional)

Huckleberry Marinade

Use this to marinate fish, poultry, pork, and vegetables, or as a simple salad dressing.

Makes 1 cup

½ cup fresh or thawed huckleberries

¼ cup red wine vinegar

½ cup olive oil

Salt and pepper to taste

Place all ingredients in a blender and puree until smooth. Store in refrigerator up to one week.

Huckleberry Chutney

A savory-sweet blend, this chutney is a good relish for grilled pork or roast turkey.

Makes 1½ cups

Combine all ingredients in a large saucepan. Bring to a boil over medium heat. Stir continuously for 1 minute and remove from the heat. Let cool, cover and refrigerate for 30 to 45 minutes. Store in refrigerator up to one week.

1 cup huckleberries

½ cup apple juice

2 tablespoons minced onions

1½ tablespoons fresh ginger, grated

¼ cup packed brown sugar

2 tablespoons apple cider vinegar or red wine vinegar

1½ tablespoons cornstarch

⅛ tablespoon salt

Pinch of ground cinnamon

Pinch of ground nutmeg

½ teaspoon crushed red pepper (optional)

Huckleberry Cream Cheese Spread

This is a wonderful spread on your favorite bagel.

Makes 1 cup

8 ounces light cream cheese

⅓ cup fresh huckleberries or 1 tablespoon huckleberry preserves

Using a mixer or food processor, blend both ingredients thoroughly. Refrigerate until ready to use. Store in refrigerator 7–10 days.

Huckleberry Festivals

During huckleberry season, July through September, there is an abundance of festivals throughout the Rocky Mountains and Pacific Northwest (and some in surprising places beyond) to celebrate and indulge in the berry sometimes called the "purple gem." These annual events include a multitude of events, from pancake breakfasts to pie-eating contests to bake-offs, music to arts and crafts, and even a Miss Huckleberry pageant. Typically these festivals occur in August, but we recommend checking locally for exact dates and locations.

Huckleberry Festival
Donnelly, Idaho

Huckleberry Festival
Priest Lake, Idaho

Potato/Huckleberry Festival (September)
Rexburg, Idaho

Huckleberry Festival and 5K Walk/Run
Wallace, Idaho

Huckleberry Festival (September)
Bingen, Oregon

Blue Mountain Huckleberry Festival (July)
North Powder, Oregon

The Mount Hood Huckleberry Festival & Barlow Trail Days
Welches, Oregon

The Swan Lake Huckleberry Festival
Swan Lake, Montana

Huckleberry Festival
Trout Creek, Montana (second weekend in August)
huckleberryfestival.com

Huckleberry Days Art Festival
Whitefish, Montana

Huckleberry Hustle and Festival (July)
Flint, Michigan

Shawangunk Mountain Wild Blueberry & Huckleberry Festival
Ellenville, New York

Castle Mountain Huckleberry Festival
Pincher Creek, Alberta

Huckleberry Horseradish Sauce

This sauce can be used with everything from prime rib to po' boys.

Makes 1 cup

Blend all ingredients in blender or food processor until smooth. Refrigerate until use. Store up to 2–3 weeks.

¼ cup prepared horseradish

¼ cup mayonnaise

¼ cup sour cream

1 tablespoon Dijon mustard

1 tablespoon huckleberry preserves

Huckleberry Candied Bacon

The salty-and-sweet combination makes this a must-try indulgence for bacon connoisseurs.

Makes 8 strips of bacon

8 thick-cut bacon strips

1 tablespoon Huckleberry Jam (see page 134)

Preheat the oven to 325°F. Coat the uncooked strips of bacon with jam and arrange them on a parchment-lined baking sheet. Cooking time will depend on desired crispness. Since ovens vary, plan to stay vigilant.

Zested Berry Medley with Chambord

The uses for this mélange are endless: yogurt, ice cream, pancakes, and much more.

Serves 4

Toss ingredients together and serve.

1¼ cups (½ pint) huckleberries (can be fresh or thawed)

1¼ cups (½ pint) fresh blueberries

1¼ cups (½ pint) fresh raspberries

1 teaspoon lemon zest

1 teaspoon orange zest

1 tablespoon black raspberry liqueur (preferably Chambord)

Huckleberry Simple Syrup

Makes about ½ cup

¼ cup sugar

¼ cup water

¼ cup frozen huckleberries

Bring sugar and water to a low simmer in a saucepan and cook until the sugar dissolves. Transfer to a glass container, such as a canning jar. While still warm, add the huckleberries and let steep. Refrigerate for up to 4 weeks. (*Note:* Strain off the berries before using.)

Resources

Bowen, 'Asta. *The Huckleberry Book*. Helena, MT: American Geographic Publishing, 1988.

HuckleberryFestival.com. (The official website for the renowned festival in Trout Creek, Montana. Here you can get the festival schedule and information for the parade, dessert contest, and fun run.)

Krumm, Bob. *The Rocky Mountain Berry Book*. Helena, MT: Falcon Publishing, 1991.

Richards, Rebecca, and Susan J. Alexander. *A Social History of Wild Huckleberry Harvesting in the Pacific Northwest*. General Technical Report PNW-GTR-657. Portland, OR: US Department of Agriculture, Forest Service, Pacific Northwest Research Station.

Index

About the Authors

Alex and Stephanie Hester have lived in huckleberry country for most of their lives. Near their family cabin in Montana, they have their own secret picking spot, where they have spent many hours handpicking berries and using them to prepare the recipes included in this book.

Both Alex and Stephanie earned their undergraduate degrees in environmental studies from the Evergreen State College in Olympia, Washington. Stephanie earned an MBA from the University of Montana.

Alex is a supervisor at a residential treatment center for children by day; in his spare time, he caters special events and private parties and enjoys experimenting in the kitchen. Stephanie has dedicated her career to natural resource conservation and currently works for the Montana Department of Natural Resources and Conservation. She enjoys eating Alex's dishes, spending time in the outdoors, music, and traveling.

Stephanie and Alex reside in Helena, Montana, with their sons, Jack and Sam.